# Driven to Succeed

## Powering Your Way to Prosperity as an Insurance Agent

### By James Brown

First Edition: August 2012

ISBN: 978-0-9858126-0-7


Printed in the United States by Morris Publishing®
3212 East Highway 30
Kearney, NE  68847
1-800-650-7888

# Disclaimers

(i) State Farm has not received or approved this material and neither supports nor endorses the material presented. Additionally, State Farm makes no warranty regarding the accuracy or usability of the information contained in this book.

(ii) While every care has been taken to ensure the accuracy of the contents of this book, the author and his associates make no warranty as to this. Furthermore, the purpose of this book is to inform and entertain. It does not constitute professional advice and the author and his associates accept no responsibility for the outcome of actions taken as a result of using the book.

# Dedication

I dedicate this book to all the State Farm Agents and Associates, past and present, who have helped grow State Farm Insurance Companies into one of the finest organizations in the world during the past 90 years.

I feel blessed to have the opportunity to represent an organization that stands behind its mission statement and strives to deliver it day in and day out. You will find no greater leader than State Farm's Chairman and CEO, Ed Rust Jr. Ed exemplifies what author Jim Collins describes as a *Level 5 Leader*.

State Farm's culture is unique compared with many of today's new companies but it has passed the test of time with honors. I look forward to continuing the journey as State Farm reaches its 100th Anniversary in 2022 and beyond.

# State Farm's Mission

State Farm's® mission is to help people manage the risks of everyday life, recover from the unexpected, and realize their dreams.

We are people who make it our business to be like a good neighbor; who built a premier company by selling and keeping promises through our marketing partnership; who bring diverse talents and experiences to our work of serving the State Farm customer.

Our success is built on a foundation of shared values -- quality service and relationships, mutual trust, integrity and financial strength.

Our vision for the future is to be the customer's first and best choice in the products and services we provide. We will continue to be the leader in the insurance industry and we will become a leader in the financial services arena. Our customers' needs will determine our path. Our values will guide us.

# What Others Say About This Book

This book is a must read. Jamie has consistently led State Farm Insurance in both Auto and Fire insurance. He has done it with proven methods and has grown a great book of business by using the methods described in his book.

**Scott Foster**, Insurance Agent – Conyers, GA

Jamie has shared the practical tools and management philosophy that have helped him reach and sustain peak performance in a highly competitive business. This is the guidebook for any agent who is ready to lose the excuses and go for greatness.

**Todd Jackson**, Insurance Agent – Anchorage, AK

If you want to learn the ways of an ultra-successful insurance agent, James Brown wrote the book, literally. His well-oiled machine has brought him to the very top of his game. If you even take a fraction of the advice in this book, your business will be in a better place. Jamie's advice has changed the way I do business and increased the production and efficiency in my office.

**Ken Phelps**, Insurance Agent – Pasadena, TX

Do you have the desire and determination to build a highly successful insurance business? James Brown has given you the recipe for that success in this book. A Must Read!.

**Al Clark**, Insurance Agent – Arlington, TX

Jamie's business practices apply to more than just insurance. I never miss an opportunity to talk business with him. I am intrigued with the machine he has built in such a competitive industry.

**Todd Istre**, Owner Southwest Dental,
Mooyah Burger and Fries,
Ojos Locos Restaurants

# Contents

# Foreword

A few years ago, I was visiting Chicago and decided to take in a Bull's game. As the gentleman next to me and I chatted, he asked me what kind of work I did. When I explained that I coached and trained insurance agents, he shared that he was a State Farm agent.

I asked him if he knew of my client, Jamie Brown. He said, "Of course, I know who Jamie Brown is. As I said, I'm a State Farm agent."

This book explains his answer to that question, as it doggedly reveals what makes Jamie the success story he is.

More importantly, this book generously reveals the process that any serious agent can follow to achieve the very same level of success.

I recently surveyed several hundred agents with the following question: "Do you feel that the world is moving faster than your agency is?" 96% said "Yes".

Many feel that the retail insurance agent is under siege. They are confused by the speed of change. Nervous about the Internet. Scared of being made irrelevant. And disappointed, in many cases, by their partnership with carriers.

Where should they look for help? Where to look for guidance? Where to look for leadership? Where to look for answers?

Over the years, many agents have asked me or members of my team if they really should pay attention to Jamie Brown. Surely, goes the thinking, he must have some "unfair advantage".

The answer to their question lies in this book. If you ever wanted a roadmap to success, why not take the same map that someone else used to reach that destination? If success is measured by being #1 among roughly 18,000 agents who represent the same carrier, how to achieve it is revealed in these pages.

Any excuses are rapidly eliminated.

Eighteen years ago, a young and hungry insurance agent became a client of mine. He was unusual, in that, at that point in time, virtually all my clients were independent insurance agents. Not this one. This curious young man was a captive agent. But he found us. And, willing to see things differently – and think differently – he signed up for the ride.

At some point, his agency was the same size as almost any agent with the ambition to read this book. Eighteen years ago, he and one full time employee were managing the entire business, and his wife's income was subsidizing the agency. Now his team of 20+ members dominates his marketplace – and stands as a beacon of hope to agents throughout America.

A word of caution. Jamie made a decision to build a world class agency. And he followed through on that decision with discipline. Day after day after day. While the strategies are clearly laid out in these pages, the decision and the discipline lie within you.

If you can dig deep inside yourself to find the passion to make that decision and to execute with discipline, you, too, will find great success.

While Jamie has called me his Business Coach for almost 20 years, I'm humbled by one remarkable truth: When Jamie speaks, *I take notes.*

Read this book. Highlight it. Dog ear it. Take notes in the margins. It's a work book. Put it to work for you. The reward is waiting.

Michael Jans
Bend, OR
July, 2012

# Introduction

This is a book about success. Not my success, but yours. It is also about a particular type of success – achieving great results as an insurance agent. This may not be the first business people think of when they consider entrepreneurial or career opportunities, but don't allow your ego to provoke a poor business decision by stopping reading.

Insurance is an immense, multi-trillion dollar business, and providing it for people in your community is incredibly rewarding both financially and emotionally.

I can confirm this because I've been doing it for more than 20 years. As further evidence, my father, my uncle, my cousins and my sister all were or are in the same business, making a great living. Now, I want to share this open secret and help others along the same route to success.

I will give you the inside information on how my office became the Line Leader in both Auto and Fire for State Farm in 2011 – a feat that has only been accomplished twice in State Farm's 90-year history. To put that in perspective, my agency was ranked #1 in sales for Auto and Fire insurance in the country, in the company with the largest market share of these categories, in the world's largest economy.

Today, we have 21 employees, a piece of business, and, in many cases, multiple policies, in 9,000-plus households and we write hundreds of applications every month (compared with an agency average of 30 to 40).

The book is for three different kinds of people. The first is someone looking for a business opportunity and wanting a realistic view of the potential of an insurance agency. The second is a new insurance agent just getting into the business or in it for less than three years. The third is someone who has been an insurance agent for considerably longer, perhaps 10-plus years, and maybe feels they have lost their edge.

This last group is the most challenged – they have most likely created a comfortable lifestyle for their families but recognize that everything in the industry now seems to be changing at a phenomenal pace.

Regardless of which group you belong to, if you have chosen to read this book, you likely are hungry for success, prepared to work hard and want to be fairly rewarded for your efforts. Those are the cornerstones of my business achievements – along with one more essential element: a great team.

I can help you achieve your success goals through insights into my experiences, the good and the bad. Although, like everyone else, I have made numerous mistakes in the past 20 years, I have also established a strong track record since being appointed an agent with State Farm in February 1992. This includes:

- Lifetime Member of the President's Club
- 45-time President's Club Qualifier
- 5-time President's Trophy Winner
- #1 in Auto – 2005, 2006, and 2011
- #1 in Fire – 2010 and 2011

If you have a positive mindset, there's no reason why you cannot also emulate these achievements using the techniques I describe.

To simplify the task, I have broken down my approach into several sets of principles, starting with some of the early lessons I learned that have stood me in good stead throughout my entrepreneurial career.

In Chapters 2 and 3, I highlight behaviors and strategies that will help strengthen performance before moving on to one of the most critical phases – building your Gifted Team. Only when this is in place, can you expand your outlook and go for significant growth that will take you to the higher levels of achievement outlined in Chapter 5.

Having the best possible team in place enables you to step back from the front line of selling, to focus *on* the business rather than *in* the business – marketing and providing the leads that support your team's performance, which I discuss in Chapter 6.

However, remember that business success is a lifetime journey. Although I am passing on to you the core of my philosophy, there are no shortcuts to avoiding the time and effort you have to invest. You should never think you've made it and you can sit back. Never think you've learned all there is to know.

I am still learning today, so the concluding chapters of the book are devoted to the process of continuous development for you and your team, with a summary of authors whose ideas have inspired me.

We live in a world of opportunity. First you have to recognize the opportunity. Then you have to learn how to convert it to success. I hope this book will help you do both.

James Brown
Annapolis, MD
July 2012

# 1

# Three Powerful Lessons

*"The most difficult thing is the decision to act, the rest is merely tenacity. The fears are paper tigers. You can do anything you decide to do. You can act to change and control your life; and the procedure, the process is its own reward."*
Amelia Earhart

It wasn't the kind of conversation-opener a ninth-grader on a ski-trip expects to hear. Kurt Riehl leaned forward slightly, looked me in the eye, and inquired: "Son, how would you like to be an insurance agent?"

If we hadn't been heading for the ski slopes, perhaps I would have jumped right off that chairlift. I had no idea what an insurance agent was, of course, except that my father and my uncle were successful and prosperous agents, and Riehl was my father's manager. But I had different ideas, so I simply shook my head.

I hardly thought about it again as a business prospect for another 10 years, for the same reason a lot of people don't: It wasn't sexy or glitzy then, and it isn't sexy or glitzy now.

Nobody grows up saying they want to be an insurance agent. So, out of sheer ignorance, many never even consider it as a career.

But here is the remarkable thing. Life as a successful agent – and I stress **successful** – offers prosperity and freedom of lifestyle choice for you and your family that are unattainable in most other careers. You have more control over your future. You get to say what you're going to do today.

I only realized this when I knew what I wanted out of life.

My higher education and career began in the United States Navy, and one thing I disliked about the military was that everyone was on a rigid pay scale that reflected their rank and years of service.

Although people rose through the ranks mostly according to ability, it seemed inequitable to me that, at any particular level, everyone received the same pay regardless of effort or talent.

When I decided to resign the Navy, I learned that the same principle applied to many business models, but I wanted to be paid for effort and results, not on how many years I had served. If I could outperform somebody, I wanted to see a financial reward.

Some people want a safety net; they want to know for sure what they'll earn every day. That is not for me. And it's not for the thousands of entrepreneurial men and women who commit to payment by results, energy and persistence – including those who choose to become insurance agents, as I did with State Farm in 1992.

In those early days, I learned three important lessons that have become part of the foundation of my way of doing business.

## Lesson #1 – Be Careful What You Say

Not everyone thought it was a brilliant career move for me. There were plenty of naysayers who considered my business location in Prince Georges County, Maryland – a predominantly blue-collar community – was a poor choice. They didn't hesitate to say so.

Perhaps I'm motivated by people who tell me something can't be done. I have never thought in those pessimistic terms about anything in life and, as I will explain later, I had done my research.

Roll forward two years from that point and, if I had been eligible (which I wasn't because I was a new agent), I would have made President's Club for the Top 50 agents in the country in Auto insurance.

No doubt I raised eyebrows with this achievement, but I'm not telling you this to boast. It surprised me more than anything that others had been so negative and dismissive. It reinforced an important lesson I subconsciously must have learned on that chairlift: Always be careful about what you say. You don't want your words to come back to haunt you.

In those early days, I also remember envious or skeptical agents who publicly and untruthfully attributed my success to getting business from my father. They spoke without knowing the facts.

The first thing they tell you in the insurance agency business is to make a list of a hundred family members and friends and insure them. I couldn't do that because my uncle and my father already had that sewn that up. Nobody was feeding me any business.

In truth, here's what really happened: 1992, you might remember, was the year of the Los Angeles riots. Although we were on the other side of the country, the riots and the underlying racial tensions were global news.

I had just opened my agency in a community that was predominantly African America, but ethnicity, language, color, religion, sexual orientation, none of those things means anything to me. I just kept my head down and worked away at building a business and a reputation, shaking my head at those agents who had spoken without knowing the facts.

## Lesson #2 – Define Your Own Success

Everyone has their own definition of success and their own reasons for striving to achieve it. Success is not what other people want for you. It is about achieving the goals you define for yourself, realizing your dreams in life and in business.

It is important to acknowledge though that, for most of us, success doesn't come easy. It calls for a powerful contribution of sweat equity. My naval career stood me in good stead for that – I was already "trained" to work the 16-hour days needed to establish my agency. In those early years, I worked 60, 70, 80 hours a week.

Nor does success come without mistakes. I had my share – opportunities missed and directions misguidedly taken. You can learn from them.

I found out one of the keys to achieving success is to identify for yourself exactly what it looks like. By that, I mean actually envisioning what it represents for you. Not the rewards but the physical shape of your business. What are your short, medium and long term goals and why? Take the time to visualize yourself at the top of the mountain you want to climb. What does it look like up there and what will you need to reach it?

What are the decisions you must make to get from where you are now to where you want to be. For example, two key strategic decisions – and we'll talk about strategy in more detail in Chapter 3 – helped grow my business enormously:

- Introducing monthly payment plans at the outset. In those days, many agents wouldn't provide them because they demanded a lot of ongoing maintenance. But they provided a powerful competitive edge when financially-squeezed customers weighed up the lump-sum versus monthly payment options.
- We went truly bilingual in 2004. More than half of my team is bilingual and that has helped us win a significant amount of business we might not otherwise have gained, while helping to strengthen customer relationships.

As an entrepreneur, I believe there are three key stages of growth that set you on the path to success.

**Stage 1** is "private practice" level. You work solo or with a small team, and acquaint yourself with every aspect of the business. This enables you to hold down your costs and learn micro-level detail. Those who are not prepared to put in that essential effort pay a high cost, including delayed profitability, and fail to lay a firm foundation for their entrepreneurial career.

In **Stage 2** you focus on building your team and beginning to edge back from day-to-day selling.

At **Stage 3** you concentrate on working *on* the business rather than *in* the business, because you have a trained, empowered and Gifted Team working alongside you.

I explore these three stages in more detail in Chapter 5.

## Lesson #3 – The Joy of Compounding

One of the vital components of my early succes
that sweat equity and those 16-hour days durir,
formative Stage 1.

Although it looks like just plain hard work, there is an
important principle at work behind the scenes.

Every minute, every bit of energy you invest,
produces a result. And if you can benefit and build on
that result – using it as a lever or platform for further
growth – your next minute, your next expenditure of
energy, will produce a higher level return.

This works in exactly the same way as compound
interest in a financial context. You invest $100 at 10%
annual interest. You earn $10. In Year 2, you have $110
to invest, earn $11, and have $121 for Year 3.

That extra dollar – $21 of growth instead of just the
$20 you'd get from simple interest, is compound growth:
interest on top of interest. And although it looks tiny, in a
few years the compound effect produces an exponential
outcome, repeated with each small task you perform for
your business.

Most successful entrepreneurs are practitioners of
the joy of compounding. It is captured powerfully and
effectively in a book, *The Compound Effect* by Darren
Hardy,[1] the publisher and editor of *Success* magazine.

He talks about the magic of showing up every day,
establishing routines and performing one small task after
another, day after day. Each element may seem by itself
to be as trivial as that one dollar. But these incremental
tasks produce a compounding contribution towards the
development of your business. The growth in the yield is
exponential.

Hardy writes: "Of all the high achievers and business
owners I've worked with, I've seen that, along with good
habits, each has developed routines for accomplishing
necessary daily disciplines. It's the only way any of us
can regulate our behavior. There simply isn't any way
around it. A daily routine built on good habits and
disciplines separates the most successful among us
from everyone else."

---

[1] *The Compound Effect – Multiplying Your Results* by Darren
Hardy, Vanguard Press, Reprinted November 2011

His book should be a basic component of your investment in a compounding return. It is also available as an audio CD; as I explain later, listening to audio recordings during downtime – when you are driving to the office, for example – is an extraordinarily productive way of increasing your knowledge and understanding.

Also, try to make Hardy's inspirational blog – DarrenHardy.Success.com – part of your regular reading.

**Key Points:**
- Nobody grows up saying they want to be an insurance agent but this business offers prosperity, the opportunity to be rewarded according to your efforts, and freedom of choice in how you run your life.
- Think twice before you speak and be cautious about what you say, so that your words don't return to haunt you later.
- Define your own success. Spend time visualizing what it looks like, and then work out in practical terms what you need to do to get there.
- Doing one small task at a time, repeatedly and as part of a routine, lays the foundation for an exponential return on your effort – the joy of compounding.

# 2

# Five Behaviors that Give You an Edge

*"When Success is shown to you, take the ticket and go for the ride."*
Michael Jans

It's one of the best-kept secrets in America but, for those prepared to work for it, the insurance agency business offers tremendous potential for prosperity, the freedom to work as your own boss, the fulfillment of leading a team to victory, and the knowledge that you are providing an invaluable service, helping to protect thousands of people.

Over the years, I have identified five valuable principles that not only help build a successful agency but also provide the tools needed to develop on both a business and personal level.

### Behavior #1: Equip Yourself for Success

Although the path to success is open to anyone, not everyone chooses to travel down it. To be a great insurance agent, for example, there are a number of core strengths with which you must equip yourself before setting out.

My list is not exhaustive but I believe you will need these as a minimum:

- An entrepreneurial spirit. This involves the drive to succeed, the willingness to take risks, the vision to spot opportunity, the grit to clear seemingly insurmountable obstacles, and the integrity and commitment to deliver on promises.

- A passion to help. An insurance agent is one of the "noble professions". This is a set of vocations dedicated to protecting and helping others, in the same way as do people in the medical and education spheres, and other public services such as the military, police, and firemen.

  You will only succeed as an insurance agent if you recognize and share this higher sense of purpose. It is also a great motivator for your team, as I learned: My Business Coach and mentor, Michael Jans, founder of Insurance Profit Systems and Agency Revolution, introduced the noble profession concept in his CSR Mastery course. When I relayed it to my team they were truly inspired by the realization of the significance of the service they were providing. Everybody wants to go to work and feel that what they do matters, that it has value and potential to make a difference. Rather than merely earning a paycheck and pushing a pen, our profession is about taking care of people and their families, and protecting their assets. We can make a difference and our advice genuinely matters.

  This is a powerful motivational message to deliver to your team. Its potential to inspire significant attitudinal change should not be underestimated.

- Thriving on failure. There are two key aspects you should know about failure:

  First, virtually every entrepreneur I know of or have read encountered failure en route to success. They just didn't let it sway them or stand in their way. They are resilient. Taking risks sometimes leads to failure but if you don't take risks, you are unlikely to achieve success.

  Second, success and failure are each functions of the total number of attempts you make. In an insurance agency, this clearly means that the more quotes you provide, the higher your absolute number of successes.

  Furthermore, in the process, of experiencing the corresponding volume of failures, each member of your team becomes more experienced, more adept at dealing with them and working through them.

The performance of a baseball player provides a useful analogy. He will not hit the ball unless he swings the bat. A Hall of Fame hitter's batting average could be .300, so seven times out of 10 he's failing! But he's also learning.

## Behavior #2: Practice the Law of Association

I don't consider myself a power-networker, but I owe a lot to the support, guidance and insight of people I have associated with over many years. It is a human instinct to group together with like-minded people, giving us security and shared sense of purpose. But this only applies up to a certain point.

If you spend your whole life with the same group of associates, never expanding your circle, never moving out of their orbit, you probably will never move on in business or career. Note that I am in no way criticizing these individuals or shunning their acquaintance. Nor am I talking about family and personal friends, though some associates may also be great friends you have known for many years. But, if you're eager and ambitious by nature and some of your associates are not, they may be holding you back. Perhaps they just do not want to step outside their comfort zone, and if you maintain your relationship with them at that current level, nor may you.

In entrepreneurial and personal development literature, there's a principle called The Law of Association. It says, in effect, that you become like the people you associate with. It even suggests that your income will probably level out at the average of the five people you spend most time with.

Looked at from another perspective, you can see that if you expand your circle and carefully select new associates you can gain the benefit of their experience, their support – and their income potential. Some of these people may become mentors, men and women who are willing to share their knowledge and ideas and to help guide you in your own personal development.

You may encounter some of them in the course of your business, but there is also value in actively seeking them out in other organizations and business groups too.

When I first started as an insurance agent, I regularly reviewed State Farm's list of top producers in my region and across the country. If I called or visited with them to express my interest and enthusiasm to learn, I always found them willing to share the benefits of their own experience.

I'm sincere about friendship and I appreciate what they have done for me. Many of them are friends for life. But, at the same time, I recognize the need to constantly move beyond that circle, outside my comfort zone, and seek yet further mentors – in other organizations and business spheres.

That is because, with the Law of Association, if you never stop learning, you never stop growing.

### Behavior #3: Use the Infinite Mindset

Acclaimed author and motivational speaker CS Hughes (www.cshughes.com), creator of the *One Minute Mentoring Program,* is a great proponent of the Law of Association and warns of the effect negative people can have on your outlook and performance.

He says: "In pursuit of becoming better, so we can enjoy success, freedom and the good life, our associations will prove critical.

"Positive people will empower you, make you feel good, and inspire your faith and confidence. They will cheer you on and give you help from time to time. Negative people are the exact opposite. They will relentlessly hammer on your faith and dreams."

As they say, "misery loves company." People who feel down want to drag you down to their level because it makes them feel comfortable that way. That was the situation I encountered with those who warned me I was setting up my office in the wrong location, that I would never manage to write insurance business in Prince Georges County .

They were so wrong. We write an average 566 applications every month.

But the difference between them and me isn't just the distinction between a pessimist, the glass half-empty individual, and an optimist, who see the glass half-full. It was and continues to be my belief that in fact there is no limit to how much you can pour into that glass.

This view is labeled the "infinite mir
something I invented, though I have
practiced it throughout my life. It is
refinement of the spirit of optimism –
limitations on thinking about what can be acl

Those with a finite mindset start from th         ... ui
believing there is only so much business to be acquired,
a ceiling that cannot be exceeded. Or, they consider that
there is one "pie" and that if someone has taken half of
it, there will be only half, a fixed quantity remaining. In
my opinion, this is simply the wrong way to look at
things. It is perfectly feasible to increase the potential
volume of business and to keep on doing so.

Here is how this infinite mindset applies:

- Just because someone else failed in their pursuit
  doesn't mean that you also will. Think of Wilbur and
  Orville Wright.
- Selling insurance is a numbers game. I know that if I
  can make that phone ring or provide a lead, there's
  more than enough business for everyone in my team.
- There really is no limit, other than time, on the
  number of ideas you can come up with and apply to
  developing your business.
- Anything is possible if you believe it is. Observe what
  other people have achieved and ask yourself: Why
  not me?

Note, however, that in adopting this approach, it is
critical that you focus on the things you can influence
and achieve. Too many agents waste time on things
they can't influence or change – actuarial rates or
underwriting rules, for example.

They'll spend hours complaining to each other about
minor issues or situations they can't control. If they could
devote that time, effort and energy to something they
can control, they would achieve a much better outcome.

Motivational author Harvey Mackay puts it this way:
"Optimists are right. So are pessimists. It's up to you to
choose which you will be." The choice is yours today
and EVERY DAY!

## Behavior #4: Earn Respect and Learn to Lead

I'm a quiet person by nature. Some people who know
me from a distance have wrongly interpreted this as

being self-centered and remote. I prefer to keep my own counsel and I have no interest in advancing my opinions for the sake of hearing my own voice. You don't have to be a full-frontal, egotistical extrovert to be a successful insurance agent.

In the same way, having a high-level job-title doesn't make you a leader either, even if you're the boss. As Jim Collins, the brilliant author of *Good to Great*[2] says, it's not that great leaders don't have egos or self-interest. "Indeed," he points out, "they are incredibly ambitious— *but their ambition is first and foremost for the institution and its greatness, not for themselves.*"

To be regarded as a leader, you need to earn respect – from your team, your peers and your customers. They don't just hand that respect to you; it is not an entitlement; you have to work for it. To do so requires time, integrity, honesty and consistency of behavior.

Earning respect is part of being a good leader and I believe that leadership is a learned skill, not a gift you are born with. Furthermore, leadership skills are not attributes you acquire in a few days, weeks or even month. They are developed over a lifetime and modified in the light of experience.

For me, nine years in the US Navy provided a solid foundation on which I have continued to build.

Here are what I consider the basic components of effective leadership:

- **Leading by example**. If you expect people to work hard, they have to see you also working hard. Although running an insurance agency gives you freedom of choice and action, if that includes a weekly 4-hour game of golf during business hours you would be sending out the wrong message. If you start and run your business on the private practice basis I described in the previous chapter, you will know how to do every job in the office, so you will never be in the position of having to ask others to do things you can't do. And if they can't do it, you will be able to show them.

---

[2] *Good to Great: Why Some Companies Make the Leap and Others Don't* by Jim Collins, HarperBusiness, 2001

- **Leadership by walking about**. You cannot lead from behind a desk or a computer monitor. You must get up from behind that desk and interact with your team and your customers. Absence can easily be misinterpreted as disinterest and a prompt for taking things easy. Interaction is an invaluable opportunity to motivate, convey enthusiasm and show you care.
- **Leadership by communicating**. You can't lead by email. Yes, there might be occasions when an electronic message is a quick way to nudge someone along on a particular task. But there's no substitute for speaking informally to each team member and holding routine meetings tailored to the particular needs of groups or individuals.

  Good communication is also as much about listening as it is about speaking. And listening doesn't mean thinking about what you're going to say next. It means truly tuning in to what the other person is saying and carefully considering their comments.
- **Leadership through persistence**. I have introduced this point already. Great leaders simply don't give up. They are resilient. You can't show weakness in the face of seemingly insurmountable challenges. Your job is to coax and show others how to overcome them – leaders teach their team or company to be resilient.
- **Leadership by delegation and empowerment**. Building on this previous point, your goal should be to teach people how to solve their own problems. Not only do you not want them arriving at your desk with questions every few minutes, you also want them to gain the sense of fulfillment that comes from troubleshooting their own issues.

  To do this effectively, you have to train them properly. Empowerment means allowing them to make judgments and take decisions based on those judgments. They won't do that if they think they're going to be called on making the wrong decisions. Accept that mistakes will happen and that your role is to guide not criticize.

  Finally, as you move to Stage 2 in your business model, you should be training the trainers – delegating teaching responsibility to your trusted senior team members.

- **Leadership through accountability**. Although you don't want a blame culture in your business, each individual has to own responsibility for doing their job to the best of their ability. That includes you delivering on what you said you'd do and acknowledging when you could have done better. When you show that you are accountable, others will more easily acknowledge and accept their own personal responsibilities.
- **Leadership through honesty**. Honesty to me is about straight-talking and not telling lies or half-truths or otherwise avoiding issues. People pick up on these behaviors and lose both trust and respect for you. Sometimes being blunt is uncomfortable but it is the quickest route to solving interpersonal issues.

  Being honest also means giving credit where it's due and never claiming someone else's credit for yourself.

Leadership is an ongoing learning process and if you weren't fortunate enough to be trained into the role, there are still plenty of ways you can pick up and develop your leadership skills.

For example, you can learn from leaders you admire. These could be mentors – people within your "orbit" whom you respect and who demonstrate outstanding leadership skills. Don't be afraid to pick up the phone and ask for their help. In my experience, good leaders are always willing to share their experience and expertise.

In addition, there is a wealth of written and audio material, ranging from biographies of great historical leaders like George Washington and contemporary thought leaders like John Maxwell, to regular entrepreneurial magazines, like *Success*, which I mentioned earlier.

Subscribe to podcasts and draw up a list of reputable blogs like those of Darren Hardy and CS Hughes. Keep a notebook or voice recorder accessible, so you can jot down leadership and success tips, ideas that worked well that could apply to you and your team, then put them into practice as soon as you can.

## Behavior #5: Know Your Team and Your Clients

I am amazed by how many agents know very little about their employees or clients or how many of their team members regard customers as merely a piece of business, a number or a source of bonus.

There is no more productive use of your time than getting to know people, understanding their needs and working out how you can meet those needs.

I previously talked about the value of management by walking about but I advise you not to do this lightly or insincerely. You should really intend to give or gain something from the experience. People are quick to spot an insincere act. Nor do they want to think you're just looking over their shoulder to make sure they're working.

It is in your interests that your team is well-motivated. They're likely to be at their sharpest and their best when they want to help you succeed as well as help themselves. Being attentive – about their concerns, their families and their interests – underscores your commitment and strengthens the bonds within a team.

It works exactly the same with your clients. Do you – or at least one of your team members – know about their birthdays, their families, the dramas in their lives, their passions? Do you let them know you know?

Here are just three effective things my agency does to maintain regular contact with clients and potential clients:

- I make it my business to chat with any clients I encounter in the office. If I don't know them, I introduce myself and invite them to do the same.
- I make myself available to talk to any client who wants to speak to me, but, if I can, I make sure I know as much about them as possible beforehand. This is an important signal of your concern and commitment both to the client and your team.
- Each member of my team sends a hand-written card to at least five clients every work day. These could be clients they spoke to that day, or perhaps those celebrating a birthday, a new car or a new home, or someone filing a claim that the employee wants to reassure they'll help them with. If you do the math: 21 employees x 5 cards = 105 cards a day, or 525 cards a week and more than 25,000 a year. That represents

full program of interaction that keeps the name of your agency at the forefront of their minds.

Nor is this simply a marketing exercise. Sometimes it echoes the "noble profession" role I discussed earlier. Perhaps one of those notes is the only personal interaction a client will experience that day, the only indication that someone cares about them. You made their day. How much is that worth?

**Key Points:**

- As prerequisites to success as an insurance agent, you need entrepreneurial spirit, a missionary sense of service, a willingness to embrace failure and an ability to anticipate and respond effectively to the good times and the bad.
- Find the courage and determination to step outside your circle of friends and your comfort zone to forge new interpersonal relationships that will support your personal development, through the Law of Association.
- Do not limit your thinking about what might be possible or let negative people drag down your aspirations. Instead, regard opportunity and potential as unlimited, and you will find that it is. Use the infinite mindset.
- You must earn respect to be a good leader. You do that by the example you set, the ways you interact and communicate, your determination to surmount obstacles, you empowerment of others, and your straight-talking honesty.
- Cultivate relationships with your employees and your clients. If you take a genuine interest in what matters in their lives, you will strengthen loyalties. And you may just make someone's day!

# 3

# Five Strategies for Success

*"I think there is something, more
important than believing: Action! The
world is full of dreamers, there aren't
enough who will move ahead and begin
to take concrete steps to actualize their
vision."*
W. Clement Stone

Some people think of strategy as a fast route to success, that if you have a strategy everything will fall into place and achievement will follow as a matter of course.

However, a strategy is merely a carefully thought-out, goal-oriented plan that most people can develop. It is the execution of strategy, not the creation of it, that holds the key to business success. Action is what counts, especially in a sales environment. A good strategy combined with an action plan that holds everyone accountable for their role makes the difference between a strategy that fails or succeeds.

In the insurance agency business, that combination of strategy and action draws on a number of key components that should form part of your approach to developing your business.

## Strategy #1: Captive versus Non-Captive

In some ways, deciding whether to become a captive or non-captive agent is partly a debate about risk and opportunity versus established brand, reputation and support.

As most readers will know (but for the benefit of those who do not) captive agents write only for one company, like State Farm or Allstate, though they may also place otherwise uninsurable Auto or Fire business in the residual markets

A non-captive or independent agent, also sometimes referred to as an insurance broker, can write for any and all insurers that they can secure an appointment with, in any and all states where they can secure a license. Sometimes, they specialize in narrow categories of insurance across wide geographical areas; they establish a niche. For instance, one independent agent I know concentrates solely on locomotive insurance.

Obviously, an independent has more possible business to go for. But the greater the opportunity, the more the risk and, often, the higher the cost. On the other hand, the more risk, the greater the potential return. Establishing a niche can give you expertise and dominance in a chosen category in certain regions of the country.

I've been a captive agent for 20-plus years and I love it for all the right reasons, including the quality of the product. I also have a brand that everyone instantly recognizes and trusts and invaluable backroom support that includes cutting-edge phone and IT systems they lease to me. I have ready-made templates for many of my business features, from emails to my website, and a regular report on the comparative performance of agents around the country against which I can benchmark my team's performance.

Most captive agents underestimate the value of the backroom support provided by their company. This support frees up a significant amount of time and resources to allow agents to focus on the primary job of creating, maintaining and cultivating relationships with their client base.

**Strategy #2: Use the Dual Business Growth Plan**
Whether you are a captive agent or an independent, there are two broad ways to grow: you can expand from within by writing new business for an existing client, or you can market your service to potential raw new clients.

Most agents and insurers do both but there's usually a tendency to favor one or the other depending on the sort of business you have. Thus, the big direct insurers like Geico and Progressive major on raw new client acquisition. The reason is obvious: They can't possibly develop and maintain the close links with individual customers that a local agent can.

Being local and community-conscious is a key strength of an agent. It makes sense to exploit that, as many agencies do, to build business by adding-on. After all, once you have a client, they likely will be with you for many years, with multiple opportunities to insure them as long as you can provide world-class service and competitive rates.

As time goes by, their lives and needs change. They get married or become a partner and there is an extra car to insure. They have children and need life insurance and college savings plans. They move to a bigger house and require more homeowners protection.

Once you have a client and if you take really good care of them, your business will grow. This is such a powerful benefit, there can be a temptation to stick with this approach as your main, almost exclusive, business focus. But, as many agents discovered when the economy collapsed in 2008, growth from within is not sustainable by itself. In the downturn, clients, like everyone else, started economizing. Or perhaps they lost their jobs or were struggling with debt. Few were buying new or additional cars.

Those agents who failed to give equal focus to acquiring raw new clients found themselves struggling. I'm not saying that they couldn't get new clients. They just had not concentrated on it, so either were insufficiently experienced or did not have the necessary processes in place to reach this potential new business.

To do that, you have to find ways to make your phone ring and provide leads to your team, which today has become one of my key roles. I make that happen through multiple mechanisms including direct mail (which I've historically used to grow my agency), purchased Internet leads from lead aggregators, and use of search engine optimization (SEO) to ensure people searching for quotes or information find me first.

SEO has recently become a core element of my strategy for winning new business, as online searches have replaced the phone book. Most people now turn to the Internet to provide the contact information they seek. They don't use a phone book; they use a smartphone. You want yours to be one of the first names they see.

That said, you should never pursue new business at the expense of your existing customer base. Established clients are still your most significant source of business, both from themselves and referrals. Research shows that word of mouth recommendations are one of the most powerful sources of business growth. If you concentrate on providing world-class service, you are not only likely to get those referrals but also to strengthen existing customer loyalty.

Never forget that if you fail to deliver the service they expect, your customers have many alternative choices and they can leave you in a matter of minutes. In the past, switching to another agent or insurer was time-consuming and hard work. Now it is not.

There are two further warnings I want to stress.

1. Dependence solely on the add-on business model is potentially a dead-end. All of our lives go through cycles of growth and consolidation. If you cultivate client loyalty, that is good, but those customers literally grow older with you. In fact, most agents' book of business is plus or minus five years of that particular agent's age.

    After the initial period of family growth, as people get older, they downsize, economize, get rid of one of their autos, sell their house and buy a condo, retire and move to another state. Eventually, they pass away.

    This is not a model for long-term business growth and you do not want to end up in your 50s and 60s with a customer base that has peaked and is now shrinking, prompting the need to start looking for raw new clients. You need to have been recruiting them throughout your working life so there is a plentiful supply of loyal, growing families in your book.

2. Inflation pushes up costs and costs push up prices, including insurance premiums. As an agent earning a fixed percentage of premiums paid, your income will go up on this basis alone (all other things being equal).

    Do not fool yourself into thinking you have it made! It

may appear a beautiful business model but this is not real growth. You may be growing revenue but you have not acquired a larger customer base or developed the skillset to find these new customers. You can't truly grow without new business.

## Strategy #3: Carefully Select Your Location
What the pessimists did not know about my selection of a business location was that I had done my homework to make sure I had a business situation that would provide the platform I needed to realize my vision of success.

Here are some of the factors I weighed up – the same ones you need to consider for your business:

- The local demographic – the population, the economic classifications and so on. You are not necessarily looking for wealth but for a population that wants to be insured and can afford to be.
- The local economy – explore all of the local economic indicators, such as the unemployment rate, average pay rates and the state of the retail market (which is always a good barometer of local economic activity). You should be looking for good diversity of employment. Be cautious if there are just one or two major employers – because your fortunes will rest on theirs.
Most relevant information is available online or from the local Chamber of Commerce or local governments.
- Limitations on risk and insurability – establish if there are factors that make some risks uninsurable – hurricanes or earthquakes for instance. This isn't always a negative, if you can write business using residual Auto or Fire markets – but you need to know this situation.
- Cost of living versus premium ratio. Premiums are high in some regions because of the level of risk and exposure. Since you earn a percentage of those premiums, your revenue will be correspondingly higher. If the cost of living – including factors like cost per square foot to rent an office, wage rates and state income taxes – happens to be comparatively low, then your revenue to costs ratio is going to be higher.

Conversely, relatively low premiums and a high cost of living make a much less attractive proposition.

- Competition. You need to know how many potential competitors are operating in your geographic area. Study their products and distribution system and determine the advantages you have over them.
- Availability of suitable office location at the right price. Location is not as important these days as it used to be. The ability to transact most business over the phone and/or Internet has diminished the importance of paying top dollar for a great location. With that said, if at all possible you should aim to be visible, accessible, and provide a comfortable office for your team and clients.

  Buy or rent? One is not necessarily better than the other. If a building represents a great real estate investment, then buying may be appropriate. Otherwise, I think you are much better off renting. Once you buy or build an office, it subconsciously limits your vision. For example, if it is 2,000 square feet and is filled to capacity with the team, most agents in this situation stop investing in their business; they have reached their maximum potential. They do not consider moving to another location – since they own their office. Put simply, renting offers more flexibility to move or grow.

- There are some solutions to space restrictions.
  - Hot-desking (team members share the same desk but work at different times). The possibility of having two different shifts for your team has become increasingly attractive. With more and more requests for quotes coming across the Internet at all hours of the day, having an evening shift work those requests is a much more affordable prospect.
  - Having team members work remotely has become much more popular over the past few years because computer technology and phone systems make this mode invisible to the client. This is only a good concept for the right team member. Technology certainly makes it feasible to work off-site – usually from home – but remote working calls for a special type of person who can remain

motivated and energetically committed to the job under their own steam.

That is not always easy, even for people who, in the office, might be thoroughly dedicated, hard workers. There are just too many potential distractions at home. In addition, remoteness from the camaraderie of the team can make the difference between a good player and a great one.

- This brings me, last but not least, to the availability in your potential location of the key people who are going to help you build your team and your business. This is discussed more fully in the next chapter but, for now, the important point is to ensure the area you are considering can provide the quality of candidates you will need to build your Gifted Team.

These key points are listed not just for the benefit of newcomers to the insurance agency business. They also provide a sound basis for reviewing an existing agency to make sure you have everything right and to question your current and future growth potential.

**Strategy #4: All Lines or Specialist?**

This is an important strategic decision. Non-captive agents have the opportunity to specialize in specific types of business. If you can carve out a niche for yourself, this could be extremely lucrative, but you will need to conduct detailed research or come from a prior specialist background to be able to do this successfully.

Many independent agents also focus on commercial insurance, representing perhaps 80 or 90 percent of their business. Commercial insurance is more challenging because of the sheer number of different types of business to be covered – contractor categories for instance, each of which requires different insurance.

On the other hand, commercial business drives a good premium and, as I have said, opens up opportunities for specialization. The only limitation is your vision – which markets you want to get into and in how many states. The growth opportunity can be huge.

For example, some companies that use captive agents have recently become more aggressive in the commercial insurance segment, encouraging captive agents to place certain commercial policies with other companies that they have an agreement with.

This can be a very successful arrangement for the agent and company, allowing the agent to maintain the relationship with the client and place the business with a carrier that has been approved by the company, thus dissuading them from shopping elsewhere.

Conversely, a lot of captive agents derive 80 or 90 percent of their business from personal lines, though they may also have certain commercial lines like habitational insurance for condos.

A different issue for them is whether to have individual category specialists within the business. I am not a great proponent of this approach as a basis for a successful and growing agency, at least as a starting point. One reason is that many agencies simply do not have sufficient business in one particular line to support a specialist.

I have two specific approaches to this issue, which work well:

First, every member of my team starts with a thorough understanding of personal lines Auto and Fire. After that, we can teach them the other lines – Life and Health and, eventually, commercial insurance. If someone wants to become a Life specialist later on, that's fine, but they have the foundation of the core business and can transition into a specialist if they have the desire and skillset.

Second, consider the potential for sharing a specialist with other agencies. There will be some management and operational challenges when sharing a team member with another office but, if you have a good working relationship with the other agent(s), these issues can be overcome. I have done this successfully with a bank/car loans specialist by choosing to work with two other agents I know well and trust thoroughly.

You need an absolutely equal split on everything – the pay, the bonus, the amount of time spent with each agency. The arrangement needs to be kept under regular review and I would say that three offices would be the maximum number for sharing. There would be too many challenges and not enough production with more offices involved.

### Strategy #5: Building Your Gifted Team

Remember that, in Chapter 1, I stressed the importance of relying on your own effort to get your business going? I'm convinced that's absolutely the best formula, both for getting to know every aspect of the business and for limiting your initial cost

Eventually, though, you reach a pivot point, a juncture where you need to set up a team to help grow your business exponentially rather than incrementally – the power of compounding again.

This is the subject of the next chapter, but it is so important – probably the most important element of your strategy, I want to stress it here. Believe me, without a Gifted Team you will never reach your full business potential.

### Key Points:

- Creating a strategy is easy. It is execution that matters.
- Captive agents enjoy the benefits of big company branding and support; non-captive agents have unlimited opportunity but with correspondingly higher risk and operational challenges.
- Growth should be founded on both add-on business from your existing customer base and a continuous influx of raw new client acquisition through lead generation.
- Do your homework when selecting an office location. Research the local economy, competition and restrict-ions on writing business. Choose your office wisely.
- If you are a captive agent, every one of your team members needs to have a solid understanding of personal lines Auto and Fire. They can specialize later, once they have proven they have the skillset necessary to be successful at selling Life and Health.
- Consider sharing a specialist with another office.
- If you are a non-captive agent and your book of business is 80-90 % commercial, consider developing a specialism in certain niches.
- The Gifted Team is the key to maximizing your business potential.

# 4

# Seven Keys to Building the Gifted Team

*"Teamwork is not a preference;*
*it's a requirement."*
John Wooden

Entertainment legend Walt Disney once said: "If you can dream it, you can do it." I am a great believer in the principle. But there is another "if" that should be added to this: If you have the right people.

I cannot think of a single business success story that wasn't ultimately built on the effort of a team. And that certainly applies to my business. If you want to build scale in your business, and have  exponential growth, you cannot do it by yourself. Drawing on the concept of compounding growth, you need a Gifted Team to propel your business forward.

What do I mean by a "Gifted Team"? Simply that If I had to leave today and was not able to come back to the office for an entire year, when I finally did come back, the business would be bigger and better than it was when I left.

That means the team has taken ownership, they are empowered, committed, accountable and driven to succeed.

Naturally, this is not a starting point. To build a team like this takes time. Members have to be hand-picked, self-motivated, bought-in to your business principles and effectively trained. To reach that point, I believe there are seven key actions you must take to build your Gifted Team.

### Key #1: Lead with Vision and Authority

A team cannot run optimally without a strong leader. I discussed leadership in Chapter 2. The important point is that if you are the agent, you are, by default, the leader. You don't have a choice, but you do have a challenge: to demonstrate your ability in this role.

A good leader shows the way, both by setting an example and by creating a sense of unity in pursuit of a common goal. A leader earns respect by showing respect, by treating employees fairly and honestly, and by acknowledging and celebrating success.

Above all, an effective leader constantly has his or her finger on the pulse of the business. The team knows it and feels more secure and committed because of it.

In his classic leadership book, *On Becoming a Leader*[3], management guru Warren Bennis says all leaders have four essential competencies:

- The ability to engage others by sharing a vision.
- Exuding a sense of calm authority through personality and self-confidence.
- Integrity, including honesty and a strong moral compass.
- The ability to adapt to the relentless pace of change going on around us.

If you start with these principles, you will establish a solid foundation for your leadership.

### Key #2: Set Targets – Monitor Performance

An important element of leadership is the ability to inspire your team to success. But what does success mean in tangible terms? What are your expectations of each team member?

With my sales team, success is defined by a "perfect day". It is our goal and our benchmark for every day, and for a sales rep in my agency it is distilled into a single, simple formula, a clear target:

### *Write 5 Applications & 10 Quotes per Day*

---

[3] *On Becoming a Leader* by Warren Bennis, Basic Books, 2009 (4th edn)

In round terms, 5 written applications per day equals 100 per 20-working-day month, plus 200 quotes, which are potential successes for the future. Our closing ratio is 30%, so, although we are not writing everything we quote, these numbers together show quite clearly what the expectation is and what each individual should be capable of producing.

The quotes represent their individual *effort* and the applications they write are the *results*. If I have a new sales team member, I'm initially more concerned about their efforts than their results. Their effort reflects their work ethic. If I'm getting the effort from them (10 quotes per day), I know we can teach them how to close 30% of their quotes, which will eventually achieve the desired result of 5 applications per day.

With customer service reps (CSRs ) that do not sell, it is more challenging to set precise targets but is still vital to monitor performance. Technology is a powerful enabler. With modern phone systems, you can monitor each CSR's hourly and daily performance and measure such aspects of their activity as the numbers of outbound and inbound calls, how long the rep was in and out of the phone queue.

We also begin each day by assigning incoming emails that need a response and beginning-of-the day calls from a compiled list. We check that each CSR actions these in a timely manner.

Whether we are talking about sales or customer service, each member of the team is accountable for their performance. Each day, I review the previous day's numbers to identify slippage or any other concerns.

I cannot stress enough the importance of monitoring performance daily. It is remarkable that so many agents have no idea from one day to the next how their individual team members are performing. Whether in or out of the office, if these agents ask for a report on how the day is going, I guarantee the response they would get is "Busy".

I have no idea what that means unless I can put some numbers to it. Defining the perfect day and seeing how close to it you came or by how much you exceeded it will tell you precisely what kind of a day it is. I cannot imagine running a business without setting the bar and seeing the immediate result.

Sidney Harmon, CEO of Harmon International Industries reportedly wrote the following in his quarterly report to shareholders: "I am fully engaged in the company. I pay attention and I know what goes on throughout it."[4] That is the way I run my business; it is my mantra.

I also continuously question if I have set the performance bar high enough. Obviously, if everybody is having a perfect day every day, I have not. This should apply not just to individual performance but also to the full gamut of goals you set for your business. If you are achieving all of those goals, the bar is too low.

In earlier times, it was common business practice to say that you should set the bar at double your current business level, aiming to clear it by working harder and smarter. If that seems to be a stretch, consider that business coach and thought-leader Dan Sullivan now believes you should set your sights on a 10-fold increase.

In today's economy, says Sullivan, double is just not enough and may even hurt your business by inhibiting the sort of growth rate you need to survive. That is a massive paradigm shift, but it is indicative of an emerging trend in business prosperity.

### Key #3: 'A' Players Only
In the long term, the most successful businesses, including insurance agencies, comprise exclusively or mainly 'A' players. These are people who:
- Learn quickly.
- Have a strong work ethic.
- Are great team-mates.
- Have a great attitude.
- Have good people skills.
- Are willing and able to take responsibility.
- Are willing to step outside their comfort zone in pursuit of growth.

They don't need an MBA or even a college degree, but they should have at least a good high school education.

---

[4] ibid

Equally important, they need to be street smart and understand your business model.

Naturally, people of this caliber rarely walk into your office and ask for a job on Day One. Recruitment is still a numbers game of hits and misses, complete with its own success ratio. I have hired people – and so will you – who are 'C' grade or lower.

This is easy enough to do because, when people interview, they are on their best behavior and you don't begin to discover their true strengths and weaknesses for at least a couple of weeks or possibly longer. This occurs even if you use a staged selection process, as I do: an initial phone interview, an aptitude test, an interview with the office manager and service supervisor, and an interview with the agent.

So to build your 'A' team you have to pursue a process of trial and error, drawing in far more applicants than you will need to employ. I have learned that an effective way of finding people to initiate this process is simply to post on the online classified site *craigslist*.

But I also have my antenna up for potential recruits when I meet people, for example at a seminar/ conference or an unrelated function, or even in a public situation like sitting in the bleachers at a school or college sports tournament.

If I meet someone who has the attributes I'm looking for, it's such a valuable discovery that I will hire them regardless of whether or not we have an immediate opening.

I am not saying that I only have 'A' players in my business. I do have a brilliant office manager and an outstanding service supervisor, which is critical for this level of the business. I also have a core of experienced 'A' players I know I can rely on. But others may still be too new to be able to identify yet whether they have the full potential we need to keep growing.

Nor am I necessarily saying that because people are not measuring up to my definition of an 'A' grade they might not be good or even outstanding in another work environment. They just might not be suited to this type of business or able to fit in comfortably with the rest of the team. If they are astute, they will recognize this themselves and look for another position. If not ...

**Key #4: Let Your Weaker Players Go**
My message to new employees is that when I hire them, I do not owe them a job. I owe them an opportunity and it is their responsibility to make the most of that opportunity. If they don't, I tell them, they will be replaced because we only have so many chairs in the office.

I don't deliver this in a threatening or intimidating tone, but, by putting my cards on the table at the outset, people know where they stand and what is expected of them.

Inevitably, there are times when people do not make the most of the opportunity. The adage that your team is only as strong as its weakest player applies here, so when an individual's performance does not come up to expectations, you have to let them know and let them go.

There are two signals of underperformance: feedback from your team, especially managers whose opinions you trust, and the numbers the new person produces.

Although you don't expect them to be writing record levels of business in their early days, you do expect to see some results and you expect to see these moving steadily on an upward curve.

Feedback on multiple levels is vital too because, in addition to delivering good results, being an 'A' player is also about attitude and people skills. This applies not just to relationships with customers but also to relationships with colleagues. A bad attitude from one player can spread like a cancer in your office.

Letting someone go is not easy for most people and, like me on occasions, you might be inclined to give them a couple more weeks. However, the feedback and your own early instincts usually turn out to be right.

When the moment arrives, I simply tell them: "I made a decision and unfortunately I am going to have to let you go." I do not go into details; they are usually well aware by that point of what the issue is.

However, sometimes you have to let people go whom you respect and who may be perfectly competent in a different environment. Perhaps they are just not gelling with your team or have skills outside of those you are seeking.

If I can help these people get another job I will. Often it might be with another agent, where they are usually welcomed because they have had the thorough training we provide. And they may go on to do great things, which is fine.

In his book *Great By Choice*[5], Jim Collins notes how Progressive Insurance has said that having the right people is the #1 strategic pillar for achieving goals. The company states proudly that "there are 15 people who we asked to leave who became presidents of other insurance companies."

I cannot match that achievement, but I can match the sentiment.

**Key #5: Give Them the Leads**
The only thing that generates new business is a prospect. That prospect may be someone who walks in through the door of your office, sends an email or Internet request, calls you by phone, or who happens to be in the market for insurance when you go out and find them.

Training obviously plays a part in teaching your team how to solicit business. So does good customer relationship management, especially in the pursuit of add-on insurance policies. But the most important sources of potential new clients are leads – inquiries you spark into action.

I am primarily focused on personal lines insurance, which is a volume business. I do not want to lose any clients but if one leaves me, even one of my bigger ones, although it is going to hurt, more mentally than anything else, it is not going to bankrupt me.

However, the loss of a client for any reason whatsoever, does underscore the fact that new business must keep flowing. That does not happen on a sufficient scale unless I move away from the switch from selling business myself to generating those leads.

This is an inevitable consequence of moving through the Three Stages of Growth I discuss in the next

---

[5] *Great by Choice: Uncertainty, Chaos and Luck – Why Some Thrive Despite The All* by Jim Collins and Morten T Hansen, HarperBusiness, 2011

chapter. Today, most my time is spent on high-leverage activities – making the phone ring, attracting leads and training my team, or training the trainers.

### Key #6: Effective Training and Practice

In his book *Outliers*[6], journalist Malcolm Gladwell helped establish an understanding about the importance of training and practice that has become known as "the 10,000 Rule."

What he discovered, or at least confirmed, was that in almost any pursuit, from playing a violin to developing technology, the best exponents, those usually regarded as geniuses in their field, all passed a landmark in the amount of time they spent developing and refining their skills: 10,000 hours.

Extending that principle, I regard repeating any business process 10,000 times as holding a key to success.

So, if a sales rep can average 200 calls a month (the "perfect day" as described above), that equates to 2,400 a year. In four years they should be best-of-class experts.

Fortunately, you do not have to wait until those four years have passed for them to reap the rewards of that experience. As with the musical prodigies and uber-geeks who put in their 10,000 hours of practice, improvement in performance is incremental and compounding. Each hour, each quote, is built on the cumulative experience of the past.

But while practice may sharpen skills, it has to be based on a foundation of formal learning and coaching.

This is why training is such a key element of building the Gifted Team, and why I started the previous chapter by making the point that it is the execution of strategy, not the creation of it, that holds the key to business success.

In an insurance agency, this requires knowledge of all the company guidelines and underwriting rules, and how to work with a client to give them the best possible price within specific parameters.

---

[6] *Outliers: The Story of Success* by Malcolm Gladwell, Back Bay Books (Reprinted 2011)

Sales reps must know what the best possible price is and the full range of options from which a client can choose.

For illustration, here is an overview of the training process at my agency:

- We break the team into groups based upon their experience.
- We use the morning time, 8:00 – 9:00 am, for training.
- My senior team members train the new team members.
- I train my senior sales reps.
- My service supervisor and office manager train the CSRs.
- I will provide additional training to certain groups of team members during the day.
- Occasionally we will have an office-wide meeting to go over important issues.
- I will also use email to notify the team immediately about important issues.

The results we have been able to achieve speak for themselves but so also do the other agents who hire people we have previously trained.

Beyond structure and informal training, however, there are certain innate talents that cannot be taught but which come as a package with the individual. For instance, with telephone skills, you might be able to help employees refine their telephone manner, but the basics – the way they verbally interact with customers on the phone – is something they have either got or they haven't.

This is difficult or impossible to teach, yet it is increasingly important because so much of business is now conducted over the phone, rather than face-to-face. The remarkable thing is that some people can be really good at face-to-face interactions but stumble badly and irrecoverably when they can't see the person they're talking to.

**Key #7: Reward Performance, Celebrate Success**
One of the key reasons I chose an entrepreneurial business life as an insurance agent was a desire to get

rewarded for my efforts. I believe the same motivation is shared by every true-grit hard worker.

However, one of the great revelations that contradicts many people's beliefs and expectations is that pay alone is not the big motivator we might think it is. Above a certain level that covers basic needs, the desire to earn more starts to slow and other factors come into play.

These factors include acknowledgment of success, job satisfaction, a great team spirit and a good working environment.

So, while it is important to be competitive on pay, and to strike the right balance (where appropriate) between basic pay and bonus, it is equally crucial to address these other issues. That's why it is imperative to monitor and manage relationships in the team and to look for opportunities to highlight and celebrate success.

This doesn't necessarily have to be fancy or expensive unless the circumstances are truly exceptional. A hand-written note shows you noticed and that you care. An expression of thanks in front of colleagues will reflect your gratitude. An informal pizza party or a suite at Minor League ball game will show your appreciation and strengthen the team spirit.

Ken Blanchard author of the business classic, *The One Minute Manager*[7], offers these valuable guidelines for giving praise:

- Be immediate; don't save it for later.
- Describe what the individual did right.
- Share how it helps the organization.
- Encourage them to do more of the same.

He says: "Help people reach their full potential. Catch them doing something right."

There likely will be other things you can do too, like contributing to a charitable cause that's important to an individual team member, as a thank-you for outstanding service and support. It will fortify loyalty.

When it comes to job satisfaction, one of the challenges is to ensure the work has enough variety and that there are opportunities for self-improvement by broadening skills and deepening knowledge.

---

[7] *The One Minute Manager* by Kenneth H Blanchard and Spencer Johnson, William Morrow, 1982

You can only write so many Auto insurance applications before they become tedious. But this can be countered by reminding your team that insurance is a people business. Filling forms is only a means to an important end: providing protection for customers.

Even this presents opportunities for variety. First, every customer is different, and second insurers are constantly revising their guidelines and rates, so even those don't stay the same for long!

**Key Points:**
- Effective leadership provides the foundation for building a good team.
- Set tough targets, monitor the results daily and keep everything under constant review.
- It may take time to find them but you only want the best players; you have to let your weaker players go.
- Support your team by generating leads and providing thorough training.
- Acknowledging and celebrating success is as important as rewarding results.

# 5

# Three Stages of Growth & Six Strength Strategies

*"Without continual growth and progress, such words as improvement, achievement, and success have no meaning."*
Benjamin Franklin

Every year, in mid to late November, I sit down with two pieces of paper – one a document I wrote the previous year and the other a blank sheet. The first reminds me of what we set out to achieve in the current year.

It allows me to review what worked and what didn't, although it will not contain surprises since I know from one day to the next how the business is performing, with daily, weekly and monthly reports. The second sheet records my goals for the next 12 months.

Goal setting and action planning does not have to be any more complex than this. Some agents have away days with their whole team, shutting their office, but I believe this is neither feasible nor necessary.

That does not mean I exclude my team from the process, but, by the time I sit down, I will have already discussed the key issues informally with them, notably my office manager and customer service supervisor. I am more concerned to know from them whether we have the right players on the team.

Their opinions are critical in deciding what we are capable of achieving or what we need to do to reach more ambitious goals. It is equally crucial to have full team buy-in to those goals, that everyone knows and understands what we have to do and has an opportunity to question or clarify the thinking behind them.

There are two essential elements of goal-setting:

- Goals must be flexible. We operate in a fast-moving marketplace and in turbulent economic times. Create goals in such a way that they can be quickly tweaked to take account of sudden and unforeseen changes.
- The three Gs: Goals Go for Growth. No matter what the market conditions, we don't want to do next year what we did this past year. We want to grow. If one sector of the market looks weak, growth must be achieved elsewhere.

The concept of growth underpins the whole structure of the business and drives our day-to-day operation. This has been my approach from the outset and reflects the previously mentioned Three Stages of Growth, which will take you from a one or two person model to an extraordinary business that you lead through vision, coaching and direction.

Here they are in more detail:

**Stage One** is the "private practice" model where most new businesses begin. You invest your own sweat equity in building a solid foundation and learning every aspect of the business. If you do this properly, expect to spend at least 60 hours a week from the outset and be prepared to learn and perform every task yourself, from taking payments to processing claims, from quoting to writing new business.

This is how I started – with just myself and a secretary. The advantage, as I have explained, is that not only do you get to know everything about the agency business basics and the market but also that you do not take on significant debt. You have total control over your finances and can make course corrections instantly. You have limited risk, thereby freeing yourself to focus on building your agency.

This is at least a five-year process during which you gradually add to your team as you grow the business. You cannot rush this stage because there is a lot to learn. For some, Stage One may turn out to be the limit of their ambitions, which is acceptable if that fits with their definition of success. By the end of those five years, you will know which direction you want to take.

**Stage Two** is where you rise to when your goals call for further expansion and growth. By this time, you are starting to build your Gifted Team – which means employing the right people, and giving them the tools and processes to help expand the business.

Now, much of your time will be devoted to recruiting, training and developing the team, focused on the twin functions of sales and service. You will be passing on your experience and expertise, so it is time for you to move away from personal involvement in sales and service.

This can be difficult because some clients insist on talking directly to you. My response is to assure them that my team members are specialists, with in-depth expertise in the particular area they are considering and that they will therefore be more appropriately served by this specialist. I am still seen to be involved in the process but not to the previously significant degree – more at arm's length.

If someone insists on discussing an issue or concern with me, I will still bring in one of my service reps to the meeting, and introduce them. I explain that the rep is going to deal with the issue but reassure the client that I am there and involved. This begins to ease them into the process of dealing with someone else.

Some team members also are reluctant to allow you to stand back. They would like you to be involved in every decision, and struggle to transition to acceptance of the empowerment you offer. For them, I compare the process and my involvement to a visit to the doctor's office: The doctor does not weigh or measure you or take your blood pressure – a nurse or assistant does that. You only get to see the doctor for five or 10 minutes.

This is a mindset issue. Your job is to make sure clients are taken care of; their job is to take care of the clients. If reluctance to accept this becomes a persistent, insoluble problem, you may have to remove such people from your team. At all costs, you must resist the powerful forces trying to suck you back into day-to-day activities.

Again, this is a gradual process, taking several years, during which you will be learning too – discovering how to stand back from the sales effort, avoid micro-managing and focus your attention on your team.

In **Stage Three,** at around the 10 to 12 year point, you have built the Gifted Team I wrote about in the previous chapter. You can concentrate on working *on* the business rather than *in* the business. It is your job to ensure that your marketing is effective in providing leads and making the phone ring for your team.

You must constantly recruit and train, hiring in advance when you identify a strong team prospect. You must reinforce the empowerment you have given to the team to resolve issues themselves. If you do become involved, coach the individual so that they know what to do next time. After that, if they dump a problem they are capable of solving on your desk, consider my technique of resolving the issue but then adding three more for them to deal with.

You want now to be able to concentrate fully on your personal gifts, which has the double benefit of making your working life more enjoyable and making the maximum contribution to the growth of the business. I count my personal gifts as an ability to envision the future and communicate it to my team, and a talent for marketing, which I will discuss more fully in the next chapter.

Both of these characteristics are essential for continuing to drive exponential growth. You have the Gifted Team who can write new business and handle customer issues, but you have to set the pace and direction – and deliver the leads.

I owe the definition and exposition of the Three Stages to my mentor, Michael Jans; it is largely the process I have followed during the past 20 years.

One word of warning: If you follow the Three Stages of Growth, you might be able to transition from one stage to the next in a shorter amount of time than I did, but you do have to progress sequentially through them to optimize the potential of your business and, as I have said, you certainly should not rush Stage One.

A lot of newer agents make the mistake of thinking they are immediately at Stage Three and skip the invaluable process and lessons that have to be learned in the earlier stages. Someone reminds them they are a

CEO and they straightaway mentally go to this final stage. Do not do that – you won't get the grounding you need, you won't get the respect of your team, and you won't get the growth you want.

Indeed, in most cases, agents that jump straight to Stage Three usually acquire significant debt, which creates additional stresses and pressure, significantly impacting their attitude towards the business.

**Strength Strategies**

Throughout this process you can leverage your growth through a number of **strength strategies** based on building client relationships by establishing a regular communication channel and by offering them a world class service at the best possible price. Here are some of the components of that approach:

**Strength Strategy #1 – Annual Reviews**

When you work at developing a good relationship with your clients you are strengthening the bond of loyalty. They know you or one of your team members on a first-name and often face-to-face basis.

You become a friend, and it is much harder to stop dealing with a friend than it is to sever links with an anonymous business. At the very least, they likely will call you if they are thinking of going elsewhere, to give you the chance of trying to retain their business.

As you work to extend your client base, it is essential that you do not, in any way, neglect those in your existing book of business. It is much easier and less costly to retain and grow business from your existing customers than to win new ones.

The core component of this strength strategy is the **annual review** process. This is something I did not do in my early years, and learned about the hard way. I would always provide a world-class service when a customer called me but I did not talk to them regularly. If they didn't contact me, I assumed they were satisfied.

This is not enough. They may well be satisfied but, without that regular contact, you are giving them an excuse to look elsewhere either for renewal of existing policies or for covering new risks for them. With an annual review in place, my clients now know that:

number one, I care about them; and number two, I'm taking care of their needs whether they choose to come in for the review or not. They know I'm not taking them for granted.

In most cases, clients choose to come in maybe only once every couple years. Then we take the opportunity to get to know more about them, to talk about their families and their interests. We are building the relationship deeper and deeper, which is something the direct writers just can't do.

It is a **differentiator**, a unique strength of an agency. After all, agents and direct insurers have more or less the same technology, but we have a completely different social interaction methodology. There is always going to be a certain percentage of people who want to work with a direct writer but, all other things being equal – including price competitiveness – a large majority of people would sooner have a business relationship with a person they know and trust.

They know who to ask for when they call to discuss their insurance issues and needs. By contrast, if they contact one of the direct insurers' call centers, they likely would be unable to reach the person they last spoke to; they may even reach a different call center.

My annual review process is now well-established and produces positive results for my clients, my team and my business. Here are the key elements:

- Every client gets a phone call once each year inviting them to come in for the review. I outsource only this part of the process. If you try to do it in-house, take my word for it that it just won't be done – something else more pressing will get in the way.
- There is no pressure to attend. Clients either decline or make an appointment, which may be for a face-to-face meeting or, if they prefer, a telephone call. I think this is going to change in the near future, as computer video technology and busy lifestyles shift the review process to video calls or at least to a phone conversation. My aim is to make it as easy as possible for the client to transact business with my office. Geographical boundaries are going to become less and less significant in the future.

- If they opt for a review, they meet with one of the more senior members of the team who is well-versed with all lines of business and with their insurance history with us. The chances are high that the client and the team member will already know each other, which makes for a comfortable process.
- We ask a simple list of questions to make sure we don't leave any gaps in protecting them and their families.
- By understanding the lifestyle of the client – for example the changing structure of the family, their responsibilities and dependents – we work with them to ensure they have the insurance coverage that meets their needs.
- An annual review should take about 30 minutes. Where that might lead into completing an application or, say, doing a Life analysis, then it may be an hour.

**Strength Strategy #2 – Long Term Value**
The enduring nature of an agent-client relationship enables you to exploit another strength strategy – **long term value.**

Price competitiveness is as much at the forefront of the consumer's mind as it ever was and there is no shortage of marketing claims from direct insurers about their ability to deliver significant savings. You would be a unique agent if you never encounter this as an argument from an existing or potential client for taking their business elsewhere.

I respond to this argument by telling clients that I don't claim to be the cheapest every six months, but that we are price-competitive in the long term. While there's no way we can guarantee we're going to be able to deliver the cheapest Auto rate at every renewal, if they bring all their cars, their home and all other insurance needs to us, they will maximize discounts. If they stay with us for 10 years and earn more discounts, like claim-free reductions, I will give them the best value over that period as a whole.

I tell my clients this and I guarantee it because I know it is true. And I tell them that just because a direct insurer claims to have cut out the "middle-man" doesn't mean they don't have to do the same work an agent does.

have to quote, write the policy and handle
d problems. They didn't eliminate the work;
ook it somewhere else.

## Strategy #3 – Inbound Calls

Some agents make the mistake of marketing their services at the wrong time. The company or companies they represent may be promoting a particular line of business, or the agency's year end may be approaching and they've fallen a long way short of one of their targets. So they hit the phone and begin canvassing potential customers, existing and new.

The call often arrives when it's least wanted – such as when the prospect just arrived home from work exhausted or is trying to get dinner prepared while the children are restless and squabbling.

In other words, these agents are trying to drum up business on their own schedule, not that of the unreceptive prospect. It doesn't endear you to them and it rarely works, which is why my agency doesn't make cold calls.

The time to talk to your prospects is when they have "insurance on the brain" – when they are calling you. You answer their question, solve their problem and then, while they are in an insurance frame of mind, you use the opportunity to explore their needs.

This isn't rocket science. You are not bothering them; they are calling you. They are thinking about insurance and you have the products they need. What is more, technology places that information right in front of you on your PC. So, for example, you can tell them you noticed that while they have their Auto insurance with you, they don't have their Homeowners. But if they did, you explain, they maybe could earn a 17% discount for the combination.

The difference is this: Cold calling is telemarketing, usually unwelcome. Making the most of inbound contact, whether by phone, click or walking into your office, is a way of offering further help and support.

## Strength Strategy #4 – Retention

I have already made the point about the value and cost of a retained client versus the cost of acquiring a new one. Every successful agent should have a simple but effective retention strategy in place. Here are three effective actions you can take:

- Communicate! The Annual Review and the regular mail-outs – five handwritten cards a day – that I previously mentioned are key elements of letting your clients know you care about them and your relationship with them. But every interaction with your clients is an opportunity to reinforce your relationship. In that case, ensure too that you are using your clients' communication method of choice – increasingly, these days, that means text messaging.
- Motivate your service reps. It is challenging but not impossible to create a bonus structure that gives your Gifted Team service reps an incentivized target of customer interactions each month. At my agency this includes not only the five personal cards but also five "grade cards" mailed out to clients every day. They must get at least five replies each month. In addition, they must fulfill a quota of client contacts from daily call sheets and email inquiries.
- Be there. Our telephones are personally answered 24/7. We use a customer response center (CRC) that can handle most issues when my office is closed.

## Strength Strategy #5 – Embrace Change

Not everything that happens in life, including your business, goes the way you want it to. The direction of change can be one of them. Do not be one of those people who bemoan change and hankers after "the good old days". Whether they were good or not, they are gone. Change is a fact of life and you better hope or even want your company to change, or else the customer is going to leave you behind.

Don't swim against the current either, even when you don't agree with technology, policy and rate changes planned by your company or companies. I speak from experience, having once decided to install a vendor's CRM database management technology in addition to the State Farm system because I happened to think the vendor system was better.

It might have been, but it was never going to work effectively outside of the organizational and technology structure of which I was part and which provided valuable support. Although I did it for all the right reasons and invested a lot of my money and time, I had to acknowledge my misjudgment and abandon it.

**Strength Strategy #6 – Dynamic Marketing**
For more on this, read on to the next chapter.....

**Key Points:**
- Setting goals need not be a complex or lengthy process but it must be based on growth, flexible enough to adapt to market changes, and be effectively communicated throughout the business.
- To establish an extraordinary business, you have to start at the beginning as a "private practice" to learn everything about the business and the market, and then gradually move away from the front line as you go through the Three Stages of Growth.
- Use the six strength strategies – annual reviews, long term value, inbound calls, retention programs, embracing change and dynamic marketing – to underpin your growth.

# 6

## Five Sharp Marketing Tools

*"The winner is the chef who takes the
same ingredients as everyone else
and produces the best result."*
Edward de Bono

The phone hardly rang the day I began writing insurance in Prince George's County, Maryland, or the days after that. And when it did, it was mainly existing customers that I took over from the retiring agent.

I didn't intend to let it stay that way. Over those early weeks, I went out and met every one of them or invited them in for a review so I could put a face to the name and begin the process of building relationships. A good start, but the phone still wasn't ringing. I tried telemarketing – the first and only time. Telemarketing in metropolitan areas is a significant challenge and it didn't work for me.

So, I tried a more personal approach, writing 25 letters to people down the street from my office. Three replied and I wrote up two of them. That was better – two new clients for the price of 25 stamps, a good rate of return.

So I began to send out 25 letters a day, then 50, then 100 and the phone started to ring off the hook. I got to the point where I had a letter folding machine in the basement of my house, and a big printer. Eventually, I was printing five or six hundred letters a day, and stuffing them with magnets while I watched Monday night football, with the help of a "junior assistant" – one of my children.

I personally delivered the trays of letters to a bulk mail center, where the staff all eventually knew me. Every week I would saturate one of the zip codes I had identified as my core potential market. I did that for 10 years, out of my house, before shifting to State Farm direct mail because they would pay for part of it with co-op dollars – and it required a lot less labor.

While many businesses have now abandoned direct mail, I still send out 300 letters a day and reap the benefits. But this early experience led to an interesting self-discovery: I enjoyed the challenge of marketing and I was extremely effective at it. As a successful agent, you must be good at it too – or you better find someone who is.

You may have learned the insurance agency business from scratch through Stage One. You may have built your Gifted Team, set your goals for growth and established outstanding customer relationships. But unless you are investing time and money in marketing – making that phone ring, or acquiring Internet leads for potential raw new clients and add-ons for existing clients – the rest is futile.

Marketing encompasses a whole range of activities that promote your organization with the aim of winning new business and reinforcing the brand. There is a lot to learn and there are many teachers. In my case, I was fortunate at an early stage to encounter one of the gurus, Michael Jans, the founder of Insurance Profit Systems (now Agency Revolution).

Time and experience are also great teachers – you learn what works and what doesn't. Here are what I consider to be the five sharpest marketing tools for an insurance agent:

**Marketing Tool #1 – The Annual Review**
I have already discussed this in some depth but want to emphasize the importance of the annual review as a regular process. Finding more sales from your book of business is probably the most frequently overlooked opportunity.

Outsourcing the initial customer contact ensures we get it done. And since they are multilingual, there are no language barriers when they make contact with my clients, many of whom are Hispanic.

## Marketing Tool #2 – Direct Mail

You know the start of my direct mail story. Today, it is expensive and, in the age of the Internet, agents and other businesses are seeking cheaper options.

Good luck to those who rely solely on online marketing and desert the mailbox. When they do, I win because there is less in the mailbox to compete with my letter for the recipient's attention. Most importantly, direct mail still works for us, with a steady and measurable success rate.

But there is an additional sharp competitive edge associated with direct mail that many overlook...

## Marketing Tool #3 – Focus on Your Marketplace

Although there are theoretically no boundaries to your geographical area of operation, the vast majority of your business will come from your locale, precisely because you are well-known, trusted and, indeed, part of the community.

Rule #1 for direct mail is never to go beyond a 10-mile radius from your office. Rule #2 is to stay tightly focused on your core area, so that you can concentrate your marketing fire power rather than spreading it thinly over a wider area.

Because direct mail is expensive and I want to achieve total penetration of my marketplace, I did a demographic profile many years ago, of which zip codes produced most of my business.

I cannot mail out to 20 or 30 zip codes, so I identified my **10 Core Zip Codes**. I started to direct mail them in 1993 and have continued to do so ever since. In effect, I am in constant communication with all the residents in those zip codes perhaps eight or nine times a year. I want to ensure a direct mail piece hits them just when the company they're currently dealing with increases its rates or delivers bad service.

I dominate these zip codes. I am branded in these areas. Sometimes a resident will eventually come into my office and start a conversation by declaring something like: "You've been mailing me for the past 10 years...." And I reply: "Well, what took you so long to get here?"

Of course, it's expensive – I've spent $100,000 a year for the past 18 years. That's $1.8 million. But it works.

## Marketing Tool #4 – Referrals

We get 15% to 18% of our monthly new business from referrals. That is a powerful number you can't argue against, especially because a good referrals system is remarkably simple to establish.

Whenever we get a new client, we let them know how much we appreciate their business and that if they have any family or friends who might need insurance to please pass them one of the business cards we give them. In return, we tell them, if they encourage the person they referred to identify them as the source, we will send the referrer a $10 gas card. We also send a handwritten thank-you note.

The note and the gas card are mailed regardless of whether we write new business with the caller, although we mostly do. After all, the original client has fulfilled what we asked them to do, and if they referred one person and feel rewarded they may well refer more.

Like everything else in our business, we track the success of referrals against the cost; it represents an impressive return.

A word of warning: Some agents use the referral process in a much more assertive way, asking the original client to provide contact details so that they (the agent) can then solicit the prospect using the referrer's name.

I don't recommend that approach; you will make the client feel uncomfortable and unlikely to provide further referrals, you will be virtually cold-calling the prospect, and you could end up souring the relationship between the client and the prospect, which in turn will damage your relationship with both of them.

## Marketing Tool #5 – The Internet

The Internet is now a multi-purpose tool. There are so many options to pursue and the pace of change is so rapid that it's vital not only to keep tabs on what is happening but also to ensure you track results so that you can assess effectiveness. Here are the key channels to consider:

- **Internet lead aggregators** harvest names of people known or considered to be insurance prospects. They use many different techniques, some as simple as running an online quote request page that users fill in. Aggregators are definitely part of the marketing mix but it is a high volume tactic – sometimes providing thousands of potential leads – and their results are unpredictable and oftentimes disappointing. I use them because they do identify prospects and I want to know about everyone in my area who is in the market for insurance.

  If you go down this path be aware of the need to manage those numbers. If you must process such a high volume of leads, you probably need to use technology – as I do, with a system called dialyourleads.com – to support the intensive phone calling and keep track of results.

- **Search Engine Optimization (SEO).** If your web page content and coding don't get your agency on the first results page of a web search for insurance in your location, you miss a massive and growing amount of potential new business.

  But doing so is easier said than done – because the search engines, like Google, Yahoo and Bing, don't tell anyone how their search algorithm works. In addition, they frequently change the algorithm and the search selection factors so that even if you manage to work out what's happening, your knowledge has only a limited lifespan.

  For this reason we outsource our SEO management to a specialist, Imprezzio Marketing, that is fully acquainted and ahead of all of these issues. The result is that we usually appear in the first three results of a search for insurance in my area.

- **Mobile display advertising.** This Internet feature throws up your corporate banner and contact information on cell phones and other mobile device screens when the user is considered to be a potential business prospect.

The approach is still in its infancy and may turn out to be more valuable as a branding tool than a direct lead generator.

We have tried it and attracted a lot of impressions but very few calls. We have discontinued it in the short term until we can identify a realistic prospect of producing a return.

- The same reservations apply to **social media marketing**, using services such as Facebook and Twitter. Many non-insurance firms, especially retailers, are already using social media successfully, but more for branding and customer service than to gain business. It is less clear that it would generate leads for an insurance agent.

  However, along with mobile technology, social media is one of the fastest growing sectors of Internet activity and, while insurers and agents are not quite sure yet how to follow in retailers' footsteps, this undoubtedly will form part of a future marketing strategy.

  I believe the social media space will help agents maintain and develop a relationship with current clients but, for now, do not count on it to drive new business.

## A Word About Costs

Many agents view marketing as an expense but I regard it as an investment. So it is all the more important that you do the following three things to maximize your return:

First, always measure and know the return on your investment (ROI). Don't just throw money at a marketing process without being able to compare the cost against the result in terms of new business. Only then can you know which are the most effective marketing tools for you and be able to detect changes in their performance that enable you to adjust your strategy.

Second, take advantage of all co-op dollars. Whether you are a captive agent or independent, make sure you're fully aware of every single marketing dollar that's available from your company/companies. I keep in touch with this throughout the year and build it into my November goals and action-planning process.

Knowing how much will be available and for what purposes helps me shape my marketing plan for the coming year. I will know what is really affordable for me to pursue. It helps keep my costs down, but I also know that if a company is willing to put co-op dollars into a particular line then that's where they are focusing their own efforts.

Third, strike a balance between the more expensive processes like direct mail and the low-cost ones such as a referral program. You never want to become dependent on just one or two sources for leads. Changes in technology and consumer habits can sweep these away overnight.

### A Word About Networking and Sponsorship
Networking can be a powerful way of getting yourself known in business circles but, from an insurance agent's point of view, that only makes sense if: (a) you have a high volume of commercial lines business – otherwise you will just be transacting on a one-to-one basis and that is an expensive and time-consuming way of doing it; and (b) you have the sort of outgoing personality that can make the most of these high-level interactions.

Remember that to be successful in business *and* enjoy the experience, you have to work with your gifts. So, if you have a penchant for networking, maybe that would be a successful strategy for you. I choose to make my phone ring in ways that I know I'm good at and that provide a sense of achievement and fulfillment.

On the other hand, I do think it is both valuable and important for your brand to be corporately active in your community. That may mean donating money to numerous causes or sponsoring school events and other community activities. Naturally, this depends on the location of your business – there are just too many schools in large urban areas but perhaps just one or two in small communities.

It is good to support the community but it is also important to invest those dollars in areas that will enable you to strengthen awareness of your brand and business.

Using the marketing approach I have outlined in this chapter has enabled me and my Gifted Team to build a hugely successful business. Your mix might be different. The key is to find out what works and what doesn't work for you and to concentrate your efforts in the appropriate direction.

Consistency and persistence will ensure these mechanisms work for you year after year. But, of course, that will only happen if you measure the outcome and prepare yourself to adapt and change when the time comes – as it inevitably will.

**Key Points:**

- Strengthening client relationships so you can find more business in your book of business is still one of the most powerful marketing tools.
- Even though it is expensive, direct mail still works provided it is concentrated inside your core area.
- Referrals can generate a large amount of new business for a relatively small investment.
- Internet marketing opportunities are growing but the jury is still out on their effectiveness for generating new insurance leads. Keep a close eye on it.
- Optimize the high cost of your marketing activities by carefully measuring the ROI, taking full advantage of co-op dollars and balancing high and low cost programs.
- Play to your strengths to make that phone ring! If networking is one of them, fine, but you don't have to do that if your strengths lie in other directions.

# 7

# Five Paths To Continuous Learning

*"Personal development is the never-
ending chance to improve not only
yourself, but also to attract opportunities
and affect others."*
Jim Rohn

M ost working days, for the past 20 years, I have driven from my home in Annapolis to my office in Temple Hills, Maryland. The journey usually takes 30 or 40 minutes each way, though, on a busy traffic day, it can run to an hour or more.

By some people's experience, this might not be a tough commute but it is still potentially a couple of hours' downtime every day. However, as I discovered early in my business career, drive time is actually a fantastic opportunity. For most of those 20 years, I have used the trip to increase my professional knowledge and business skills by listening to audio recordings of best-selling books.

When I started out, at 28 years, fresh out of the military and never having owned or run a business, I was maybe a little naïve and definitely inexperienced in this arena, so I did everything I could to reach out and grab business knowledge from every source I could. Learning the lessons and acquiring the knowledge of world class experts every day turned out to be one of the biggest blessings of my 20-year career – I have studied more than enough to gain a PhD in business and marketing!

This activity is a key part of my passion for continuous learning and improvement because I firmly believe that leadership and business acumen are not assets you are born with. They can be learned both through self-teaching from media like audio books as well as directly from the experts themselves.

The process never ends. There are always potential nuggets to be gained, lessons to be learned, with every figurative turn of the page. Anyone who says they know everything there is to know either about insurance agencies or the business world in general is guilty of self-deception. And anyone who ignores the opportunity to add to their knowledge and understanding is guilty of self-neglect. They will never achieve their true potential.

The trouble is that the process of continuous learning is a challenge amid the hectic whirl of day-to-day business activity. It is human nature to become comfortable with where you're at, especially if you've already had any kind of success in what you're doing. Why push harder?

It's very easy for an agent in that situation to coast along for several years before waking up and realizing that the world has moved on and passed them by. When you are coasting and you are not in this continuous learning mode, you simply are not maximizing your business opportunity

In a competitive and rapidly-changing business environment, it is absolutely imperative to improve and educate yourself about new approaches to business and marketing, advances in technology, leadership and team-building. Just think back 10 years to realize how much has altered in the way we communicate, acquire information and transact business. That pace of change is accelerating.

Listening to audio recordings is just one of the key routes to personal advancement and the development of your Gifted Team. Let's run through a broader list.

### Continuous Learning Path #1 – Books
Every week sees the publication of scores of new books on business practice. These days, they come in multiple formats:
- Traditional printed books – still a mainstay and easy to share with employees and colleagues.

- EBooks, which have the advantage of being portable, simple to store, searchable and easy to highlight.
- CD recordings – fairly portable, great in the car, good for multitasking.
- Downloadable MP3 recordings – for example from Audible.com – particularly useful for high portability on airplane flights.

You can also get abridged versions of books, both in audio and in text summaries, hard copy and digital. In other words, everything you need to know is out there in one format or another. What you have to do is seek it out and make a commitment to study.

I choose mainly to use CDs because I either don't have the time – this was especially the case when my family was young – or the inclination at the end of a hard day, to read. It doesn't matter, though, whether you read or listen but you definitely need to plug-in to this wealth of expertise.

Of course, there is a myriad of "reading" material choices. Just peruse the business section in your library or bookstore. So it is important to be able to select wisely, knowing which are the most relevant and effective.

I discuss some of the best authors in the next chapter but you can easily learn which are the new books and authors to follow. My key sources for this information are my subscription to *Success* magazine, regular emailings from Amazon.com. and word-of-mouth recommendations from other agents and business acquaintances.

You can also check out Amazon's business best-sellers directly at http://www.amazon.com/Best-Sellers-Books-Business-Investing/zgbs/books/3 or review the equivalent New York Times business bestseller list at http://www.nytimes.com/2011/01/02/books/bestseller/besthardbusiness.html

What you will find, as I have done, is that many books deliver similar messages, especially in the broad arena of business and leadership skills. But this is no bad thing, for three reasons: first, repetition has the value of reinforcing learning and strengthening understanding; second, slight nuances give you different perspectives and encourage questioning and reviewing; and third, some authors will resonate more with you than others – you will simply find it easier and more enjoyable to discover and learn from them.

Don't forget too that magazines are an invaluable source for extending your knowledge. I have already mentioned *Success* magazine, but there are others. You can't get them on CD but some are available as MP3 downloads and many as digital text (for example, via www.zinio.com).

## Continuous Learning Path #2 – The Internet

The Internet has rapidly become a fabulously rich source of learning. For instance:

- Webinars – online presentations or interactive forums. These are increasingly common and may be targeted specifically at insurance agents or a more general business audience. Many of them are free – you simply have to pre-register.

  Generally, they last about an hour – a massive saving compared with the time and cost of attending a similar real-world event.

- Podcasts – a useful supplement for audio-learners. Compared to books on CD and MP3, podcasts, also usually in MP3 format, tend to be brief – 15 minutes or so – and informative, focusing on a single issue. Some of them, though, are very amateurish and ill-informed so, again, you need to research and select carefully. Find podcasts on iTunes or just via a web search. Sample them and subscribe to the ones you feel you can learn from.

- Blogs – from latest information about business techniques and insurance industry happenings to expressions of personal opinions on trends and events. There are thousands of blogs. Again, sample them and bookmark only the ones that usefully add to your knowledge. Many blogs offer a subscription, either directly via email or through RSS feeds, enabling you to dip into them when you wish.

- Social media. It feels like they have been around forever but social networks such as Facebook, Twitter and LinkedIn are still relatively new. You can exploit them for advancing your personal knowledge by following individuals or companies you admire.

Sometimes, postings will lead you to full-blown articles.
- News alerts. Use a search engine such as Google to set up a news alert on a key word or phrase (example: "business tips") and receive a daily list of links to relevant articles and postings.
- Video presentations. Many organizations and business experts run their own channels on YouTube ( e.g., *One Minute Manager* author Ken Blanchard – see next chapter). For thought-provoking and wide-ranging discussions on the leading edge of life sciences and business, check out the global video conference and presentation service, ted.com.

As my list suggests, this wealth of information carries with it the danger of overload. There truly is so much, easily-accessible knowledge out there, that you need a plan to manage it effectively and to avoid becoming side-tracked with time-consuming and unproductive web-surfing.

You must be selective and tightly disciplined. If something is informative, that's fine. If it's entertaining and informative, even better. If it's just entertaining, drop it.

### Continuous Learning Path #3 – Workshops & Seminars

Attendance at workshops and seminars is invaluable, provided you take the right approach. They are not social occasions (though there may be a social dimension) but, used wisely, opportunities to improve your knowledge and gather intelligence from others.

They go beyond passive reading or listening by allowing you to question and clarify, drill more deeply to mine areas of weakness or special interest and to forge links with individuals who can help to strengthen your skills.

Captive insurers often organize seminars and work-shops with leading keynote speakers, but whether you're captive or independent I also believe you need to step outside of your immediate zone of familiarity to discover new thinking and broaden your own outlook.

## Continuous Learning Path #4 – Coaches and Mentors

The greatest athletes have coaches to help them improve their performance, so why should we be any different? But, if it is important for every business executive to have a coach, finding the right one can take you through an expensive and time-consuming exercise that may eventually lead you to question the value. The test of a good one is when they have been retained by the same client for five or 10 years!

In a search, the two challenges you will encounter are potential personality clashes and lack of specialist knowledge. The personality issue is down to your own instinct and you should definitely not proceed with someone whose approach or manner you find uncomfortable.

The knowledge side is more tricky. There are phenomenal coaches out there with a wealth of experience and understanding of non-specialist business and leadership skills, from whom you can learn a lot. They can help you build your Gifted Team, for instance. But the chances are they will know little or nothing about the insurance marketplace.

That was my experience a few years ago, when I ended up "coaching the coach" – teaching two coaches I had hired about the insurance agency business, a process that took me six or nine months. And I was paying!

My good fortune, however, as I mentioned earlier, was to discover someone who was both business and marketing expert and insurance marketing guru – Michael Jans. I first attended one of his "boot camp" seminars in Atlanta back in 1993 and, over time, developed an ongoing one-to-one relationship as well as continuing to attend his seminars and workshops.

The advantage of working with an industry specialist is that you are interacting with someone who is also coaching and supporting hundreds of other agents. He becomes a sort of clearing house for intelligence in the insurance agency world – he may see something coming down the pike that I may be totally unaware of yet because he's learned it from another of his clients.

I always want to know about the next big thing in the insurance agency world, so, although I have tried working with other coaches, I find myself coming back to an industry and marketing expert from whom I know I still have a lot to learn.

**Continuous Learning Path #5 – Sharing Knowledge**
Continuous learning and personal advancement are not just about you. They also are about developing your Gifted Team. As an insurance agent, you have a great opportunity to pass on the knowledge and expertise you have acquired – an action that will benefit both your employees and your business.

Captive agents, of course, are able to draw on the training support provided centrally – in the form of literature and videos. Increasingly, the flexibility of the Internet in providing instant online streaming of corporate training, available 24/7, has become a valuable component of basic sales and service training, especially for new recruits and, perhaps, Stage One agents. It may also be possible to seek local training support from an area sales executive.

But all of this is likely insufficient for a growing and growth-based agency (and, of course, for independents). It is essential to build on this foundation by developing training and messaging customized for the needs of your business.

I outlined my training program in Chapter 4. As part of this, for the first 18 years of running my agency, I also organized daily briefings for my entire team, at the start of each day. The sessions were not lengthy, but the frequency of those morning meetings was invaluable for imparting up to date information and ensuring consistency of messaging and approach; everyone knew what everyone else was doing – an approach I carried through from my Navy days.

You want everyone on the same page, but it's amazing how quickly they will fall off without that frequency of gatherings. I also found it helpful to share some of the wisdom from those great business books by playing extracts at some of these meetings.

We still do those meetings today but with a segmented structure. As the business grew, it became increasingly obvious that individual needs and skill levels were different and it was impossible to encompass everyone's requirements in a single session. Some people had been with me for nine or 10 years, others for less than 30 days.

Also, as part of my strategy to move back from the front line to focus on the business rather than in it, I passed the baton for some training tasks to my office manager and service supervisor and, in 2012, embarked on developing a full-time trainer. That doesn't mean withdrawing entirely from training – personal involvement is important for establishing and reinforcing your business philosophy – but, typically, more that 50 percent of a training session will be done by one of these key team people.

Naturally, that implies a requirement to train the trainers – from informally sharing knowledge and experience and providing guidance to hiring business coaches to develop their skills, which I did for a year or so. The rationale is simple: I want them to run the day-to-day operation out of my office, and I really want my team members to look at them as the go-to people. This empowers them, provides more challenge and fulfillment, and allows me to step back and identify where we are underperforming and the corrective action we might need to take.

These five paths provide you with the means to continuously advance knowledge and skills – yours and your team's. It is an ongoing process. I still attend Michael Jans' workshops. And I still listen to audio books on my daily commute. To me, learning is a work in progress. It is never finished.

It is not an inexpensive process. The cost of books and magazines can add up to a significant sum and workshop/seminar attendance can be a costly item. Look on it though as an investment – and something you can share and come back to whenever you want. It produces a compound return.

**Key Points:**
- Continuous learning and improvement is a lifelong process. Without it, you will never achieve your full potential.

- Books and magazines are available in the format that best suits your needs. Audio books create an opportunity to learn during otherwise unproductive time.
- The Internet is a super-rich source of information – but there's so much of it you must develop a plan to manage it selectively and effectively.
- Workshops and seminars provide an opportunity for two-way interaction, to question and clarify.
- Everyone needs a coach or mentor but business coaches are most effective for broader skills. For more effective guidance, find someone who knows the insurance agency business.
- Sharing your knowledge not only helps to advance the development of your Gifted Teams but also strengthens their performance to the benefit of your business.

# 8

# A Thousand Points of Inspiration

*"Nothing will work unless you do.*
*Get to it and GO BIG!"*
Maya Angelou

Malcolm Gladwell, the previously-mentioned best-selling author of books like *Outliers,* tells a story about the comparative achievements of NFL players based on their performance in the Wonderlic aptitude and intelligence test. It turned out that their eventual accomplishments bore no relationship to their Wonderlic result – or if it did, it was an inverse relationship. Three of the five worst scorers became Hall of Famers, while none of the top five did.

What is going on here? Gladwell believes that the difference was that, because they didn't score so well, they had a greater internal drive to succeed and prove themselves. This resolve to push gave them an edge, and it is my belief that creating an edge, driven by determination, is the key ingredient of success. You don't have to have the highest IQ to reach the pinnacle of your chosen career; you need the most drive. As an insurance agent you don't even need to invest a significant amount of money – there's no inventory or services you have to pay for upfront – to give yourself an edge

Here's the amazing thing: The real edge you need is so slight, so fine, that it's simply down to you to choose whether you seize it or not. It costs nothing. In his book

*The Slight Edge*[8], Jeff Olson emphasizes t
making decisions that may affect your entire
business success is simple – it's easy to de
something and it's just as easy to decide not to
example, it's easy to decide to work-out at the ὑ
it's easy to decide not to work out. You know whἱ    ..ᴅ
is better for you but you still have to choose.

Olson's point is that it's making those positive
decisions repeatedly, day in and day out – simple things
that I do like showing up for work, doing a day's work,
building my Gifted Team – that bears the fruits of
success. Success breeds success. It generates the
compound return I spoke about at the beginning of this
book. You are not being asked to do anything
extraordinary but you are being invited to be consistent
and persistent in the basics of building your business.

I encountered Jeff Olson, like so many other
business experts, in my car on the 40 minute commute
to Temple Hills and virtually every one of them has been
an incredible source of inspiration. There must be a
thousand of them by now. You name the book or
motivational speaker and I have probably heard him or
her.

I'd like to introduce you to a selection (it is no more
than that) of the best, some of whom I have already
mentioned, as well as outstanding commentators,
presenters, public speakers and experts, or simply
observers of life, whose opinions are worth listening to:

- **Tony Robbins** (1960 – ) Ranked among the Top 50
  Business Intellectuals in the World, Robbins is a
  motivational speaker and author of *Unlimited Power:
  The New Science of Personal Achievement.* He has
  been a featured speaker at the TED conference
  referred to in the previous chapter.
  Inspirational quote: In essence, if we want to direct
  our lives, we must take control of our consistent
  actions. It's not what we do once in a while that
  shapes our lives, but what we do consistently.
- **Pat Riley** (1945 – ) Like many sporting greats,
  basketball coach Riley has much to teach us about

---

[8] *The Slight Edge: Turning Simple Disciplines into Massive
Success* by Jeff Olson, Success Books, 2011 (Revised)

other aspects of life that draw on the skills and fortitude on which sporting achievement is based. Which is why he is also a great off-season motivational speaker.

Inspirational quote: There are only two options regarding commitment: you are either in or you're out. There's no such thing as life in-between.

- **Jim Rohn** (1930-2009) A college dropout and former Sears stock clerk who became a wealthy entrepreneur, motivational speaker. Author of such classics as *7 Strategies for Wealth & Happiness* and *Five Major Pieces to the Life Puzzle*, which defines the components of success as Philosophy, Attitude, Action, Results and Lifestyle.

Inspirational quote: Don't join an easy crowd; you won't grow. Go where the expectations and the demands to perform are high.

- **Jim Collins** (1958 – ) An academic turned business guru, Collins has authored half a dozen memorable books including *Good to Great* and *Great By Choice* , is a regular contributor to business magazines and a highly-rated speaker on the topics of sustainability and growth.

Inspirational Quote: It is impossible to have a great life unless it is a meaningful life. And it is very difficult to have a meaningful life without meaningful work.

- **Ralph Waldo Emerson** (1803-1882) I guess everyone knows Emerson, but who has actually read his great essays like *Self Reliance, Experience* and *The Conduct of Life*? He comes from another era but he still has a lot to teach us.

Inspirational quote: Do not go where the path may lead, go instead where there is no path and leave a trail.

- **Vince Lombardi** (1913 – 1970) Another of the great sporting figures who provided as much inspiration off the pitch as on it. Lombardi only wrote one book – *Run to Daylight* – but was the subject of several others including his son's interpretation of his leadership style, *What It Takes To Be #1.*

Inspirational quote: Winning is not a sometime thing; it's an all the time thing. You don't win once in a while; you don't do things right once in a while; you do them right all the time. Winning is a habit. Unfortunately, so is losing.

- **Stephen Covey** (1932 – ) Best-known as the author of *The Seven Habits of Highly Effective People*, one of the top-selling business books of all time, Covey is a charismatic speaker on the subject of principled leadership. His blog ([www.stephencovey.com/blog](www.stephencovey.com/blog)) is a must read.

  Inspirational quote: Every human has four endowments – self-awareness, conscience, independent will and creative imagination. These give us the ultimate human freedom... The power to choose, to respond, to change.

- **Zig Ziglar** (1926 – ) The master of salesmanship, Ziglar started out as a US Navy man during World War II and has been on the motivational speaking circuit for more than 40 years. In 2012, he co-authored his 13$^{th}$ book, *Born to Win: Find Your Success Code*.

  Inspirational quote: If you can dream it, then you can achieve it. You will get all you want in life if you help enough other people get what they want.

- **Edward De Bono** (1933 – ) If you want to learn how to take a different perspective on problems and challenges, De Bono is a great place to start. Author of an incredible 40-plus books, including *Six Thinking Hats*, he developed the term "lateral thinking" and is an expert on the use of language in communication.

  Inspirational quote: If you wait for opportunities to occur, you will be one of the crowd.

- **Ken Blanchard** (1939 – ) His book, *The One Minute Manager,* is the ultimate guide to business efficiency, which explains why it has sold more than 13 million copies. But Blanchard has also written 30 other books. He has his own YouTube channel, an iTunes app called How2Lead, you can follow him on Twitter and Facebook, and he blogs at howtolead.org.

  Inspirational quote: In the past a leader was a boss. Today's leaders must be partners with their people... they no longer can lead solely based on positional power.

- **John Maxwell** (1947 – ) Author and speaker Maxwell demonstrates an amazing ability to uncover and explore a huge range of business and leadership topics in the 50-or-so books he has written, including *How Successful People Think* and *Leadership 101*. He has spoken at the annual National Agents Alliance conference.

Inspirational quote: A man must be big enough to admit his mistakes, smart enough to profit from them, and strong enough to correct them.

- **Harvey Mackay** (1932 – ) For pure entertainment as well as fascinating business insight, Mackay takes some beating – as some of his book titles suggest, like *Beware the Naked Man Who Offers You His Shirt* and *Dig Your Well Before You're Thirsty*. He's also a highly-successful businessman and has his own YouTube channel.

  Inspirational quote: Time is free, but it's priceless. You can't own it, but you can use it. You can't keep it, but you can spend it. Once you've lost it you can never get it back.

- **Orison Swett Marden** (1850 – 1924) – He was a hotel owner, a writer and a philosopher, but Marden is also considered the instigator of the modern success movement in the United States. He founded *Success* magazine and, although his books like *How to Succeed* and *Ambition* are somewhat dated, they still provide useful direction.

  Inspirational quote: We make the world we live in and shape our own environment.

- **Darren Hardy** – Entrepreneur Hardy was a protégé of Jim Rohn and, as well as being editor and publisher of *Success* magazine, runs his own blog, posts on Twitter and Facebook, and authors books such as the previously-mentioned *The Compound Effect*. He is one of my major sources of inspiration and motivation.

  Inspirational quote: The people with whom we spend our time determine what conversations dominate our attention, and to which attitudes and opinions we are regularly exposed.

There are, of course, many more. If you read or listen to these great figures, my advice, as with so many other aspects of my business practice, is to do so repeatedly. I will often re-audition a book I heard maybe three years previously. It is amazing how much you gain from this – you find you understand more about the points being made, and remember them so you can apply them more effectively in your business.

Like me, you will also encounter particular comments and quotations that are especially relevant to your business or personal outlook. I encourage you to note these down (not while driving, of course!). Ultimately, you will have compiled a collection of quotes and pearls of wisdom, a distillation of important business principles that you can refer to regularly for inspiration.

In this book, I have shared some of those I consider among the most meaningful and inspirational.

### Failure As Inspiration

I wrote about thriving on failure in Chapter 2. I am serious about this. Although this book is about success, I am a great fan of failure. One is not the counterbalance of the other. In fact, I'd go as far as to say that failure is an important ingredient of success because it has so much to teach us. I embrace failure as an opportunity to learn and improve. Of course, if you don't see it that way, if you regard failure as a nail in the coffin, then that is precisely what it will be.

One of my inspirational heroes is Michael Jordan. He is not a hero because of his basketball skills per se but because of his attitude towards accomplishment and, in particular, towards failure in his sport.

In his early days, he was cut from a basketball team because he wasn't making the grade. In that situation most people would quit but he just carried on trying, learning, improving, and eventually becoming one of the best basketball players ever. But he's never stopped striving to improve and learning the lessons of failure.

This is what he says: "I've missed more than 9,000 shots in my career. I've lost almost 300 games. Twenty-six times I've been trusted to take the game-winning shot and missed. I've failed over and over and over again in my life. And that is why I succeed."

In other words, he just never gives up, nor stops trying to improve on his performance.

**Key Points:**

- It is as easy to decide to do something as it is to decide not to do it. The choice is yours.
- Giving yourself an edge provides the pathway and the determination to achieving the results you want.
- Drawing inspiration from great authors and business experts will strengthen your focus and your skillset.
- Keep a note of quotes and advice that resonates with you and use them to build a motivational collection.
- Learning from failure is an important ingredient of achieving success.

# 9

# Conclusion

*"Life's battles are not always won by the faster or stronger man – but sooner or later the man that wins is the man who thinks he can."*
Jim Rohn

I am proud, honored and privileged to have achieved a high level of success in the unglamorous world of the insurance agent. Furthermore, although it may not be sexy or glitzy, it is both potentially lucrative and tremendously fulfilling for those who choose to focus on success. Here is why:

- I have the opportunity to work with a great team of people.
- Together we provide a needed and valued service to the public.
- I am rewarded in line with the effort I contribute to my business.
- I learn and improve every day.
- There is no limit to what we can achieve.

Some people believe there's a magic ingredient, a secret sauce, that flavors my success, but it's nothing more than repeating a simple formula every day, never saying "I won't do that today" just because I don't feel like it. I am busy exploiting the compound effect. I find out what works and I do it over and over.

This opportunity is available to you

However, how you choose to realize this opportunity is crucial. The steps I have outlined in this book are my way of doing it – and the results speak for themselves. If there is any magic, it is in knowing what you want to achieve, keeping your eye on that goal and marching resolutely towards it.

In other words, you must start out by creating your own definition of success and then put in place the components that will help you achieve it – knowing your market and your customers, building the Gifted Team and leading by example, exploiting your personal strengths and committing to continuous learning, stepping outside your circle of friends and your comfort zone, concentrating your energy and creativity **on** the business rather than **in** the business, and constantly keeping your finger on the pulse of activity – all day and every day.

Above all, the most important thing you can do to ensure your success is to adopt the infinite mindset and believe in yourself. Remember this classic Apple Computer ad from 1997?

> *"Here's to the crazy ones. The misfits. The rebels. The troublemakers. The round pegs in the square holes. The ones who see things differently. They're not fond of rules. And they have no respect for the status quo. You can quote them, disagree with them, glorify or vilify them. About the only thing you can't do is ignore them. Because they change things. They push the human race forward. And while some may see them as crazy ones, we see genius. Because the people who are crazy enough to think they can change the world, are the ones who do."*

Why not you? Good luck.

# Acknowledgments

L earning is a lifetime process and I hope I have made clear in this book my debt to the scores of authors who accompanied me on my daily commute to my office and contributed so much to my self-education process.

I have singled out some of my favorite or most influential authors in the book but the truth is that every book I have read has provided an opportunity either to learn or to question.

But my indebtedness extends way beyond this rich source of support to embrace the contributions of colleagues and leaders at State Farm, who have provided support, opinion and advice over my 20-plus years in this business.

I want also to thank the employees who have accompanied me over parts of this incredible journey to success at my office in Temple Hills, Maryland. I am privileged and honored to have my own truly Gifted Team and I have gained from them as much as I hope they have from me.

I would especially like to recognize my Office Manager, Amy Copenhaver, and Service Supervisor, Alma Perez, for their hard work and dedication towards building and leading our Gifted Team.

At a personal level, I owe so much to the mentoring and support of Michael Jans and his team at Agency Revolution (formerly Insurance Profit Systems). Over the past 18 years, Michael has become much more than a Business Coach – he has become a true friend and mentor.

Above all, I would like to recognize and thank my family for the endless support and happiness they have provided to me. I truly believe a person becomes a product of their environment. So, thank you to my parents, Jim and Angie Brown, who sacrificed and provided a nurturing and loving environment for myself and my 4 sisters. Dad would always tell me: Somebody is going to do it – Why not you? And to my beautiful wife of 26 years, Kate, who has blessed me with four lovely children, Mimi, Bridget, Chase, and Meredith – may they find their passion in life and never be afraid of failure!

9/22/19